Theresa and Jonathan Hewat both worked on the fringes of the advertising world before setting off on their record-breaking, round-the-world journey in January 1973. Theresa was with a design and publishing company in North London, and Jonathan was a founder-member of a graphic design group in Swiss Cottage, London. Theresa, having completed a BA course as a mature student at the Bath Academy of Art, is now working as a freelance designer/illustrator. Jonathan is a freelance broadcaster in both local and network radio.

They set off on the journey described in this book in their almost-new VW Microbus and, living in it continuously, drove around the world completing the 89,565 miles (143,305km) through 56 countries in 3 years 4 months. They now live in Bradford-on-Avon, Wiltshire.

Overland
and Beyond

Theresa & Jonathan Hewat

Roger Lascelles, Cartographic and Travel Publisher

3 Holland Park Mansions, 16 Holland Park Gardens, London W14 8DY Telephone: 01-603 8489

Publication Data

Title	Overland and Beyond
Typeface	Phototypeset in Compugraphic English 18
Photographs	By the authors
Printing	Kelso Graphics, Kelso Scotland
ISBN	0 903909 13 8
Edition	This fifth, September 1981
Publisher	Roger Lascelles, 16 Holland Park Gardens, London, W14 8DY.
Copyright	Jonathan and Theresa Hewat

Distribution

Africa: Enquiries invited

Americas: WestCan Treks, Edmonton (Alberta)
Bradt Enterprises, 54 Dudley St., Cambridge,
MA. 02140 U.S.A.

Asia: Hong Kong — The Book Society, G.P.O. Box 7804
Hong Kong Tel: 5-241901
India — English Book Store, New Delhi

Australasia: Australia — Lonely Planet Publications, P.O. Box
88, South Yarra, Melbourne Vic 3141
New Zealand — Caveman Press, Box 1458, Dunedin

Europe: GB/Ireland — Available through overland agents
and operators, specialist map re-
tailers and all booksellers with a
good foreign travel section.
Italy — Libreria dell' Automobile, Milano
Netherlands — Nilsson & Lamm BV, Weesp
Denmark — Copenhagen - Arnold Busck,
G.E.C. Gad, Boghallen
Finland — Helsinki - Akateeminen Kirjakauppa,
Keskuskatu 1
Norway — Oslo - Arne Gimnes/J.G. Tanum
Sweden — Gothenburg - Gumperts/Esselte
Lund - Gleerupska
Stockholm - Esselte/Akademi Bokhandel
Fritzes/Hedengrens
Switzerland — The Travel Bookshop,
Seilergraben 11, 8001 Zurich

Contents

Foreword

The journey that Theresa and I completed in June 1976 took us into the Guinness Book of Records, having beaten the previous record by 20,000 miles.

The first edition of **Overland and Beyond** sold out within two months of publication. Subsequent editions (four) were gradually improved, but the essential quality of the book remained unchanged because the information it contains does not date with the passage of time.

Having sold the last few copies of the fourth edition, we decided to call it a day. By then, Theresa was a mature student of design at Bath Academy of Art, and I had started a new career in radio broadcasting in Bristol.

However the orders kept coming in and so, when Roger Lascelles invited us to expand the book and produce a 'major new 5th edition' we finally agreed to accept … and this is it.

As I've already stressed many times, no book eliminates the need for individual research according to each potential traveller's needs/requirements/money/route.

What I believe we successfully do is twofold:
1) Point you in the various right directions through the incredible maze of mis-information and ignorance that clouds the overall objective of having an unbelievable amount of FUN.

2) Encourage the toe-in-the-water brigade to take the plunge, by being as objective and truthful as possible.

Finally, I can honestly say that if you adopt the golden rule of overlanders all over the world — that **nothing** is impossible, and you take off in whatever direction you fancy, and if you heed the fairly intensive amount of advice on the following pages, you will be guaranteed an experience that will change your attitudes to people, life, and yourself to an unforgettable degree.

Bon voyage — because if you take this book to heart, **you'll go.**

Introduction

On a grey day in January 1973, our red VW Kombi trundled down the Archway road, through the centre of London, and out onto the Dover road. We were grossly overloaded, weighing slightly under three thousand kilos (3 tons) and, as we took our last look at the familiar sights, we both wondered if we and the vehicle would make it... We were not planning to get to Spain for a two week holiday, but to drive right around the world, living in our camper for at least a couple of years.

In fact the journey took three years and four months. It was the greatest experience of our lives, although we had to learn many a hard lesson due to the almost total lack of reliable and accurate information about overland travelling.

Before our long trip, neither of us had been outside Europe apart from one week in Morocco. This time we were plunging in at the deep end by heading for the Sahara. We knew that the Sahara was dangerous; highly so if you treat it casually. But what we could not find out at that time was if it was **possible** to cross it without four-wheel drive. No one was prepared to commit themselves positively. The AA said that four-wheel-drive was definitely necessary, and the RAC told us that some of their 'contacts' had got across in some very strange vehicles.

Used, by now, to this lack of information, we headed South, and were reassured by other travellers who had come North across it. Yes, it was possible, provided we had enough fuel, water, and equipment for getting ourselves out of soft sand.

It was so great to be 'on the road' at last, after many chaotic months of preparation. Many had been the night when one or other of us would wake up in a muck sweat, having dreamed of throbbing drums in the pitch black jungle night, and the cracking sounds of breaking twigs as the marauding primitive tribes approached our van, smacking their lips in anticipation of a good meal of English stew. (The dream would end just as the frantic scramble into the driving cab revealed a totally flat battery ...)

Landslides, earthquakes, hurricanes, sandstorms, floods, disease, starvation and death. Was this what we were heading for? Would we end up as prey to hoards of South American bandits — if we ever got that far? Would we die of hepatitis in India? Or thirst, due to the late discovery of a leaking water tank, in the Sahara? Were we really out of our minds like Great Aunt Molly had said?

No. We were on our way to see fantastic sunsets, ornate and ancient temples, unbelievably primitive tribes, and weird religions. Ahead of us lay noisy colourful bazaars, magnificent waterfalls, strange foods, and, above all, friendly generous people who know nothing of thermo-nuclear energy and air conditioning, but who have not forgotten how to smile.

As the days, then months, and eventually years rolled by, and we became increasingly experienced in the art of overland travelling, we often wondered if others had had similar problems in tracking down information. They had. And so, on the last leg of our journey, from India through Asia and back to Europe, we decided to publish this book with advice and answers to some of the many hundreds of questions which, for us, remained unanswered until we were actually on the road.

Absolute objectivity has been our aim. No two journeys are or can be the same, and so we have tried to eliminate how 'we did this' or 'we took that'. Unless stated as such, all subjective opinions have been heavily pruned, as this is the great weakness of most travellers talking about their journeys. They all tend to forget the normal day-to-day 'fun' things, and indulge themselves in horrific stories spiced with a fair dollop of exaggeration. Once you are on the road, you'll meet it, often.

Having successfully negotiated a horrible bit of slippery mud strewn with large boulders that is laughingly called a 'road', you meet another traveller coming towards you. Stopping for a chat and exchange of information, you apprehensively enquire what lies ahead ... "Christ! It's dreadful." He replies. "Are you hoping to get through in **that**? You haven't a hope. There's a bridge down about five kilometers from here, and you have to drive along a river bed for quite a distance. A Land Rover bust its chassis on that stretch a week ago, I heard, and if I were you I'd turn back and go another way — if you can find one ..."

What do you do?

Of course you go on. By now you've learned how to filter the truth from the ego-trips, and when you get to the part he was telling you about with such enthusiasm, you discover it isn't half as bad as the bit you'd already come through before you met him.

There are no short cuts to planning your own trip. Individual research and preparation cannot be avoided. You will find no single source (including these pages) for all you need to know. Distance, time, budget, and climates will dictate both how and where you go as well as what you take with you. All printed information giving prices or road conditions will be out of date long before you have even read it. Where we have included some prices, they are usually accompanied by dates to serve as a reminder that inflation is still rife. As US dollars and the metric system are the common language for all overlanders, they are used in this book.

Whether your proposed journey is relatively short (a few months) or a long one covering more than one continent, it should make little or no difference to the advice in these pages. However much you plan and prepare, you will, like everybody else, make plenty of mistakes, and will frequently learn from other travellers. Some live in mobile pig-sties, and others deck themselves out with lace curtains and plastic flowers. Some set off with dramatic messages painted all over their vehicles, while others cover far greater distances in quiet anonymity. Whatever you decide to do will probably have been done before, but it will be unique to you and, as an overlander, **not a tourist,** you are sure to have a ball.

1. The Idea

1.1. Why?

Before rushing off buy a toothbrush, a vehicle and a tankful of gasoline, think why you want to travel in your own vehicle. Why choose this often cramped and sometimes uncomfortable means of transport? Flying on a charter is cheaper and quicker if the main objective is your ultimate destination. Paying for an organised overland tour will relieve you of most of the responsibilities you will have in your own van. A sea cruise, though quite costly, could get you there in style. Do you relish the idea of living in a small box for weeks, months, or even years in order to travel when and where you wish? If you do, then stop dreaming about it and do it. It is the most fabulous way to explore a country or continent.

1.2. Where?

What kind of travelling do you want? There can be no doubt that the route through Asia to India or Australia is the easiest. It is also the most popular, as the roads are generally good and there are relatively plenty of facilities. You will also meet large numbers of fellow travel companions of all ages, shapes, sizes and nationalities. The scenery can vary between mountain passes, high plateaux, humid jungles, dusty deserts, enormous lakes and lush valleys. In the Far East you will find more traditions, cultural interest and exotic religions than in any other part of the globe. Nevertheless, on this route (particularly in India) you will often be driven to distraction by the behaviour of the people on the roads — with or without vehicles. Border-crossings are also more hassle than anywhere else.

If you prefer a 'pioneering' sort of adventure, with less emphasis on culture and history, then Africa is your continent. Provided the constantly-changing political situation permits the trans-Africa journey, you will find the toughest and most spectacular desert in the world, the torrid and primitive jungle, the Rift-valley mountains with the incredible wild life of East Africa, and the 'civilised' luxuries of the (whites only) good-life

10

in Southern Africa. You will also experience by far the worst roads in the world. In Africa you will be fighting a continuous running battle with the giant forces of nature, and it can be very exciting indeed.

Perhaps the continent that offers most, however, is America. From North to South, or vice versa, there is an unbelievable variety of scenery, cultures, people and sights, in whatever proportions you choose according to your route. You can fight your way up a pot-holed road to 4,800 metres (15,750 ft) in Peru, or glide along the San Diego freeway in Los Angeles among up to fourteen lanes of traffic. There are glaciers in Southern Argentina, the mysteries of the Inca civilisations in the Andes, primitive tribes in Ecuador and the Amazon basin and the incredible impact of the Iguassú falls. There is also the mind-blowing Grand Canyon or the fun of Disneyland. New York, Rio de Janeiro, Quebec or La Paz, it is all there and, as the guide books say, much much more ... It is still impossible to drive (without the help of helicopters) between North and South America. A short but expensive sea-journey to or from Panama is necessary, and will be for several years to come. Maybe this is a good thing as the two sub-continents are kept so totally different while being physically joined together. With the addition of Central America, the mixture (in our opinion) cannot be beaten.

We did not visit Australia but believe, despite cries of protest, that for the overland traveller this continent has the least to most expensive to reach direct from Europe. This viewpoint is elaborated on pp 64 & 65.

1.3. When?
Timing your journey is very important. To try to cross the Sahara in August is as insane as to travel through Eastern Turkey in January, or Zaire in October. The best months to visit India are October through February, thus avoiding the over-powering heat of the summer months and the rain and floods of the monsoons. It is not too difficult to find out climatic conditions for the countries you intend to visit, from the relevant foreign embassies or other organisations such as the Met. office. If you plan an extensive journey, criss-crossing the equator several times, it will be almost impossible to adhere to ideal weather conditions all the time. However, local weather should be given careful consideration if you are to enjoy your journey to the full.

1.4. How?

Budget pressures may tempt you to consider sharing the vehicle between two or more couples. In fact the size of the van may be chosen with this in mind as one way of reducing the potential costs of the trip. Our advice is, if at all possible, *don't* do it. It can work out, but very rarely does. The best and closest of friends at home always end up fighting like tigers or splitting up, long before the journey is over. With just two people you can have a much more workable unit.

If there are four of you, two small vehicles in convoy will give you the freedom to go separate ways at times, and meet up again later. Free-camping is easier and safer with more than one vehicle but, of course, your fuel costs will be proportionately higher.

The cry "I'm much too old for that sort of game, alas!" is nonsense. There are old-age pensioners on the road as well — in one instance visiting Pakistan in a three-wheeler car. We encountered a party of four Americans in two VWs in the central African jungle and the **youngest** of them was just 72 years old.

Many families travel with their children and/or a pet or two. The children can quite definitely gain enormously from the experience, but conversely may lose out by missing a more 'normal' school life if education is done by using a correspondence course. The decision is a very personal one.

1.5. Miscellaneous

Endless general tips and information could be passed on under this heading, but the sensitive traveller will pick these up as he goes. Keep an open and constantly curious mind, and don't be afraid to tap all possible sources.

A few intriguing examples: In Thailand it is considered extremely rude to pat someone's head or to point **with your feet,** while in India you should **never** proffer your left hand — the one which, with water, is used instead of toilet paper. To fart in Afghanistan is a great insult, and can get you into serious trouble if it's a noisy one. One of our friends was forcibly ejected from a shop for this unhappy breach of etiquette, though he escaped lightly if the story that another traveller had both his ears cut off for a similar offence is true.

12

It is good to travel with some small gifts. You will surely need them. The poorest of people will often surprise you by their kindness and generosity, and you may frequently want to reciprocate. Simple things for more primitive or out of the way areas, like matches, foreign coins or some stamps, cheap T-shirts, ball-point pens, small mirrors, postcards or illustrated magazines and of course sweets for the kids are a few ideas. We saw one imaginative idea proudly displayed on the wall of a South American border post: a small flag containing a message 'Thank you for helping us on our journey through your country. John & Sylvia Jones, Brighton, England.' embroidered on it.

In Iran, among other strict Moslem countries, the weekend begins on Thursday afternoons and Fridays are the equivalent to Western Sundays with many places, and all offices closed. Saturdays and Sundays are normal working days.

As you travel East or West, there will be continual half-hour or hourly time changes. These are usually, but not always, effective at frontiers. There are also some odd calendars: In Japan, for example, the date 31 March 1976 is often written 'Showa 51.3.31' while in Iran, the same date would be written '31.1.55' — the new year beginning in March, and '55' being the equivalent to '76'.

You may not be a collector of things under normal circumstances, but on an overland journey it is worth thinking about collecting small lightweight items such as coins, stamps, matchboxes or similar things either as a gift for someone on your return or as a souvenir of your journey.

Before we set off, we recorded our impressions of what the journey would be like. The food, the people, the customs, the scenery, what we would miss most, etc. It was funny and interesting to play back once we arrived home ...

2. Africa: the dark continent

Although the purpose of this book is to serve as an aid to prospective overland travellers through the planning stages of the forthcoming trip, there must be a considerable element of curiosity about the journey itself. For that reason I've decided to include this, and the next two chapters on our own particular story as a departure from the otherwise predominantly **objective** content. It may serve as an appetite-whetter. It may stimulate alternative plans. But above all it will hopefully illustrate the kind of life than an overlander can expect to enjoy wherever he or she intends to go.

If this section of three chapters was the principal part of the book, it would be a travel-adventure book and, like nearly all of them, the author would be tempted towards exaggeration and drama. Overlanding isn't like that. Of course there are plenty of exciting moments. And there are times when one feels more than a little scared by a potentially hostile world through which one is travelling. But those moments are always the tiny minority set against a life of absolute freedom, exquisitely beautiful and truly unusual scenery, and continual contact with basically very simple and amazingly generous local people.

On our journey around the world, my wife and I began by heading South from Britain — seeking the sun and warmth as a contrast to the grey drizzle of Northern Europe in the depths of winter. Our inevitable choice was the dark continent: Africa.

In just two chaotic weeks of European motoring, in the cramped over-stuffed van, we were on the small ferry that took us across the Strait of Gibraltar which separates two chunks of land that might be a thousand miles apart.

The noise and chaotic bustle in the Moroccan cities was very bewildering at first, but we gradually tuned into the totally different atmosphere in the air. The laughter; the shouts; the clanging bells; and the clattering hoofs of the horse-drawn carts. Beggars surrounded us, and small boys continually pressed us to come with them on tours or to see some 'special' sight. It was already hot, and the stench from open sewers mingled with the smoky fumes of grilling camel meat.

The stalls lining the narrow streets were piled high with an enormous variety of leather and metalwork or other handicrafts for the ever increasing flock of tourists and souvenir-hunters, and every now and then, there was a stall full of the most utterly hideous luminous coloured plastic junk for the local community.

An ancient white bearded head emerging from a crumpled pile of white cheesecloth material at the foot of a wall offered to share some food with us: revolting chunks of raw flesh which he carried in a glutinous lump in the hood of his cape. He also proffered a strange drink of blackcurrant juice. Beggars, often maimed, everywhere. A circle pressing around a boxing match in the street, or listening to a storyteller. We wandered through the old towns with their intricately carved doors, and came across huge vats of brilliant red dye for staining the strong-smelling leather skins.

Always pressure. Always tension. Always laughter in the air. First, Rabat; then Meknès; and then Fez. The cities merged into one another and our minds boggled at this, our first impressions of the dark continent ...

The roads were good, and even in the remotest parts, they were often lined with small boys selling a huge variety of foodstuffs: eggs, carrots, celery, oranges, fish, rabbits, asparagus, cactus fruit, tortoises, snails, chickens and camel meat. We were on our way.

Northern Algeria greeted us with torrential rain and incredible thunder storms. We were beginning to feel the giant forces of nature and the immense power of this ferocious continent.

The British Embassy in Algiers seemed so tranquil and orderly. We went there to enquire if it was *possible* to get across the Sahara without four-wheel drive. "They're bound to know" we assured ourselves. "They're only 300 miles North of it ...

We went up to the enquiry desk, and spoke to one of the officials.

"Good Morning"

"Good morning. We're hoping to drive down to Nigeria, and wanted to ask if it's possible in a VW Camper. We've tried to find out in London, but no one was prepared to commit themselves, definitely, about crossing the Sahara."

The official handed us two forms which we had to complete — including the names and addresses of our next of kin. We pressed the question. "Well," was the dubious reply, "I've been to the *edge* of it, and looked at it. But I don't know anything about getting across it ..."

Our only real assurance came from other travellers we met in Northern Algeria. We would spot their battered-looking Landrovers, laden with jerry cans, and sand ladders, and would anxiously approach them for advice and information. Yes, it was possible, provided we had adequate fuel and water stocks plus the equipment for getting ourselves out of the soft sand. We had.

Over the Atlas mountains — through four feet of snow — and along the ribbon of beautiful smooth tarmac that stretched like an arrow, south towards the shimmering heat of the Sahara.

The compass held steady, due South, and the stumpy trees and scrubby parched bushes began to thin out. Fewer donkeys and goats. More and more camels. Children looking after their animals waved and called out to us. We were nervous, and excited.

At night, on the outskirts of the small towns or villages, we would find a reasonably secluded spot to camp. Often, the only secluded spot, near enough to the town for us to get help if attacked, was the local rubbish tip. But it was usually quiet.

On several occasions, having eaten our evening meal in the cosy security of our new home, there would be a rap on the side of the van. Pitch dark outside, and with the curtains drawn, we felt trapped. Heart thumping, I'd call out *"Qui est là?"* and there'd be a mumbled reply in a dialect I couldn't possibly understand.

"Qu'est-ce que vous voulez?" I'd enquire, and out of the jumbled tangle of words, maybe spot a few I recognised. *'Parlez'* ... and *'cadeau d'oranges'* and a few others. Cautiously, I'd peer out and see an Arab with a gift in his hands. Some oranges; a cup of camel's milk; two or three eggs. We'd struggle to talk for a while in school French. Some others would arrive, and we'd sometimes chat for hours about *'Les Beatles'* or The Queen and London, while the mosquitoes and bugs poured in through the open door.

16

"Like forgotten galleons floating in a vast sea of dust" the gigantic rocks rise up out of the Southern Sahara in Niger. This was the spot where we spent 1½ days immobilised by a ferocious sandstorm.

17

This was our first taste of the kind of people we were to meet all over the world: Simple, friendly people; curious about any strange foreigners, and prepared to give even the smallest gifts as a token of their friendship. But without the slightest inkling of the meaning of the word 'privacy'. They would assume that they were wanted and would have no idea that we might, at times, wish to be left alone after the pressures of a hard day's driving. The VW was a magnet to them, and they would stare in wonder at the luxury of the interior, stuffed so full of things **we** considered essentials, and which they considered the most outrageous luxuries.

All too soon, the beautiful smooth surface of the new asphalt road came to an end, with a mighty bump, we were onto the beaten track of tyre marks that would hopefully lead us across the one thousand seven hundred miles of dusty barren waste that is the greatest desert in the world.

By now, the asphalt road stretches all the way to Tamanrasset, though the possibilities of its continuing much farther South are somewhat remote, as roads from 'last towns' to borders are notoriously poor all over the world, and Niger to the South is unlikely to be involved in any kind of elaborate road-building scheme in the North of their Country for many moons.

So Tamanrasset is the spot where 'the men' continue South, and 'the boys' turn timidly back ..

The first third of the Sahara was the Tademait Plateau. High, and not too hot. The surface was predominantly stony. Sharp stones that threatened to cut the tyres to ribbons. The tracks of the vehicles that had gone before fanned out, each seeking a smoother patch, and trying to avoid the corrugated surface of the well-worn track. The horizon shimmered in the distance; flat, brown, and parched, like a burnt waffle.

Suddenly, we came to the edge of the plateau. It dropped like a cliff into a huge basin of dust, and we stood on the edge of the steep slope and gazed into the distance in awe. Already, the grossly overloaded roof-rack had partially collapsed, and I tried to strengthen it and remove some of the heavier gear. Then, down we went on the winding narrow track. Slithering on the loose stones, we crawled slowly round the hairpin bends. Far below, we could see a large trans-Sahara truck grinding its way up, with a plume of dust floating behind it.

Now, at the bottom, we felt the blistering heat of the Sahara burning down on us. But it was a dry heat and, with the windows open and the natural air circulation of the moving van, it was not too unpleasant. Only when we stopped for a bite of lunch did it hit us with its full force. We ate little, and drank gallons. The corrugated ('washboard') track chewed up our heavy-duty shock absorbers — and our nerves — with equal voracity. After several hours of these hideous vibrations, we'd leave the track and drive beside it on the smoother surface of the desert. But, inevitably we would pay the price: a hidden patch of soft sand, lurking in wait for us.

Sinking up to our axles, we'd grind to a halt. Brute force would sometimes get us through if we had enough momentum, but usually the patch was too big, and we'd have to dig ourselves out. There were various procedures: scraping the loose sand away, placing a sand-ladder under each wheel having jacked the van up, and gradually working our way out to the nearest firm surface. Or trying to drive out on half-deflated tyres which give more grip to the drive wheels. In the furnace conditions, which-ever method we chose (and there were various others) we soon learned that the only way, once we had left the track for a brief respite from the vibrations, was to stop as soon as we saw a 'suspect' patch, no matter how small it appeared to be, and have a look on foot. It was tedious, but it worked.

By the time we reached Tamanrasset, the most Southerly oasis town in Algeria, we had become quite expert, but still fre-quently became bogged down in the more cunningly disguised patches. It was good training for the tougher stretches yet to come.

Set like a brilliant green emerald in a huge golden platter, the lushness of the oasis palms seemed incredible. As we drove into the dusty bustling streets, hordes of flies descended on us like bees to a honeypot. The brown, mudbrick houses that lined the main street were shaded by tall trees and it was cool ...

A local welder tried to repair the damaged roofrack, and we stocked up with cooking gas, water, bread (of sorts) and a few tiny and very expensive eggs and tomatoes. The water was strictly rationed, and it took two patient hours to fill one two-gallon container from a dribbling tap.

Now, we were heading for the deep Sahara. South of here there is the toughest part of the desert with the tiny oasis town of In Guezzam and the frontier between Algeria and Niger. Before we got to Agadés, a fairly large oasis town in North Niger, we would be very much on our own. Up to now, we had had to report in to each oasis and give the local police our expected time of arrival (to nearest day) at the next. The theory was that should we fail to arrive, a search party would be sent out to find us. But having experienced the Arab attitude to this sort of bureaucratic arrangement, it was probably only a theory. However, the track between Tamanrasset and Agadés crossed the border between the two countries, and neither country seemed remotely interested in people who were crossing that frontier. The Sahara is exquisitely beautiful. The purity and the isolation are quite mind-blowing, with ever-changing colours; reds, browns, ochres and yellows, and knife-sharp jet black shadows. It's cruel and savage, and demands respect. You feel tiny and insignificant.

In the Tamanrasset area, there is a range of mountains called the 'Hoggar' Mountains. These are giant jagged peaks, reaching up into the deep blue above like black claws. A lunar landscape, so pitiless and harsh — and yet so truly awe-inspiring. They are well worth the detour from Tamanrasset on the top road through their most spectacular peaks.

Almost every day, the scenery would change ever so slightly. Some times it would be almost entirely rocky, with pebbles and boulders littering the entire area. Then there would be vast expanses of fine yellow sand, with the huge dunes, or 'ergs' like mountain ranges stretching into the distance. Then there would be the days when we would travel through a mass of flat-topped hills of rock and sand that seemed to dance on the silvery pools of water that changed to sand as we approached. Sometimes, we would pass between enormous mountain-like boulders of solid rock that seemed to float like long forgotten galleons on an abandoned sea of dust. It was a magic place. A place of such utter isolation and deafening silence that it remained one of the highlights of the long journey that lay ahead of us.

During the nights, we would lie on our backs on the still-warm rocks and gaze up at the myriad of sparkling jewels in an inky black velvet setting — just an arm's length away. We often played a tape of Vivaldi or Albinoni on the cassette player and the purity of the baroque music seemed totally appropriate to the environment.

We quickly realised that the Sahara desert, which took 3 weeks to cross, is often very stony, as shown by the surface we had to drive on for several days in S. Algeria.

Our routine, after a somewhat chilly night, would be to get up and have breakfast before the sun came up. Then, as it shot up over the horizon the blistering heat could be felt sweeping over us and we'd set off. This kept the van cooler for longer, and gave us a good head start.

At the border (which we took some time to find) we were travelling with two other vehicles: A Landrover and a beachbuggy — with the Landrover humping all the buggy's supplies. Our passports were duly filled in by hand as the soldier had no luxuries such as a rubber stamp. It took ages, and one of the party went off to the nearby well to top up with water only to find a very dead dog floating in it. We hoped that the well on the other side of the border would be in rather better condition.

It wasn't much better, but we all had adequate water supplies and so we sat around and debated whether or not to take the main track due south, or to believe the rumours we'd heard, of a much better route off to the East to a mining town called Arlit, and from there South to Agadés.

It was a gamble, as the tales one hears are often untrue. Yet we all knew how awful the next bit of desert would be if we stuck to the track marked on the Michelin map. The one to Arlit was not marked on the map at all, but on the other hand, we'd heard that two young Frenchmen had died in this area the previous year, having broken down on what they believed was the correct track and sat and waited for help. Being the wrong track, none came, and they died the most terrible death of all ... thirst. So, since then, the route to Arlit was said to be clearly marked with beacons. But could we be sure?

The beacons that are meant to mark the entire track across the Sahara have almost completely disappeared. They comprise (when you do see one) either a large pile of stones like a cairn, or a large oil drum with a pole stuck on top. Even if they are spaced out every kilometre, it's often very difficult to spot them through powerful binoculars, as the mirage effect breaks everything up into a mass of dancing shapes. Two French couples in a pair of sturdy 1933 Dodge Military ambulances painted all over with black and white zebra stripes came up just then and joined in the discussion. It was amazing to find so many 'foreigners' in one spot in the Sahara, and we all enjoyed the impromptu conference immensely. It was agreed that as there were five vehicles, we'd take the risk and head for Arlit.

It turned out to be a wise decision. The virgin desert was superb to drive on, and we rarely got stuck in soft patches. When we did, we towed each other out, and there was a beacon almost every kilometer of the way.

We left the two ambulances in Arlit, as there was a French community there with all kinds of facilities including a bank and, believe it or not, a full size swimming pool. Maybe the two French couples are still there ...

Apart from all the normal day-to-day hazards of crossing the Sahara, there are others like a freak sandstorm which can blow up out of nowhere and sometimes last for days. It's impossible to see more than a few metres in front and the only thing to do is to stop and sit it out, hoping the van won't be buried, or the track completely covered.

We encountered only one, and that was enough. It lasted for 1½ days, and we sat in the van thinking of strawberries, and ice cream, and chilled white wine, and melons and other succulent dishes while the wind whistled and howled outside, and the sand blasted against the side of the van.

The Southern Sahara certainly lived up to its reputation of being extremely tough, and our VW went through a fair amount of punishment. Although we still hadn't had a puncture since we left London, we had used two complete sets of shock absorbers, and the third set was on its last legs when we pulled out of Agadés on the last major leg of the desert crossing. This meant that we bounced up and down over the humps of sand across the track like a ship in a storm.

About eight miles South of Agadés we were trundling merrily along when we came upon three neatly spaced drifts across the track. We hit the first and it threw our nose up into the air like a jet taking off. We crashed down just in front of the second which threw us up even higher. The third welcomed us with open arms, and we sank into it like a stone into a mound of marshmallow, and were brought to a standstill in a split second.

After we'd extracted ourselves from the piles of debris that had flown from the back of the van to the driving cab (the typewriter included) we got out to inspect the damage. Instead of being parallel, the two front wheels were almost at 90°. One track-rod had acquired a sizeable elbow, and the van was immovable ...

Luck was definitely on our side on that day, as the disaster had happened only just outside Agadés, and there was a strong chance another vehicle would appear quite soon. Had we been deep in the desert, we might have had to wait several days for one to come by. Sure enough a military jeep came past within a couple of hours, and we were literally dragged back into the dirty noisy fly-ridden town and within a few hours the local blacksmith had hammered our trackrod back to a recognisable shape again.

From then on, we never tried to 'ride' the corrugations at speed again. We took it slowly and were shaken and rattled until we felt that the fillings were falling out of our teeth.

And then ... we saw a small scrubby bush. And then another. And another. The desert was beginning to end. It was an immense relief to see those bits of stunted twisted growth. And yet, it was also a sad moment as well. Mixed with our feeling of elation that we had succeeded in getting ourselves across, reasonably intact, was a sorrow that we would probably never experience such incredible, rugged, grandeur on such a magnificent scale again.

Within a day or two, we began to see camels and goats. And the little huts of the nomadic families who looked after the animals. The people of Niger were negroid, and the children would dance with excitement at seeing us. They waved, and rushed towards the van screaming with joy through glistening white teeth. "Araaaab! Araaaaaaaaaaaab!"

It took some time for us to gather what they were shouting. We were pale skinned, and from the North. We were Arabs. Arabs from the desert. It made us feel great. After three and a half weeks, we had finally done it. The first leg of the journey was over, and we felt elated. We were Arabs from the desert ... .

What could be more extraordinary than driving out of one extreme, the yellow-brown barren wilderness of the previous three weeks crossing the Sahara, into the lush tangled rain-forests of central Nigeria? The asphalt roads were reasonably good despite the many potholes, and the resulting speed accentuated the contrast even more.

We were refreshed from a few days stopover in Kano, a large city in the north of the country where we had found the 'Kano Club' and its fabulous swimming pool. We'd nearly killed ourselves from sunstroke giving the entire interior of the van a complete clean-up, and we were now all set to cross from West Africa to the East coast through the unbelievable density of the Central African rain forest.

But first we headed south to Lagos, that putrid, steamy, noisy, smelly, humid melting pot. We fought our way through the suicidal drivers who seemed undeterred by the crumpled remains of cars, vans and trucks that littered the side of the roads. Every vehicle seemed to have been commandeered by the local populace. Bulging with humanity, inside, outside and on top, they screamed along in a determined race with death. In one of the accidents we saw, a small Peugeot pick-up van had collided with a vast petrol tanker. From that one accident there were no less than 26 people killed.

Almost all the local vehicles, which should, by rights, have been in the nearest breaker's yard, were highly decorated with bright colours and little lights. And above the windshield, a wonderful assortment of slogans in Arabic, Hausa, or English: 'God is God' 'Envy no one' 'Let them say' 'All for money' 'God first — all roads' 'James Bond' 'Try and see' 'Yours sincerely' and, on one crumpled wreck that would never move again from the ditch it had careered into: 'Shall return'.

The English language was frequently murdered in the most charming way. For example, at an Esso filling station which provided the service of key-cutting during the first half of the day, was a sign which said: 'MORNING KEY CUTS AT ESSO HERE'.

Lagos meant our first mail pick-up point. It was fabulous to sit in a cool air-conditioned cafe and pore over the mass of letters from home. We wandered about the 'posh' part of Lagos; the Marina, and Victoria Island, and saw the beach where public executions are held. Walking into the plush Bank to collect our money was like walking into a refrigerator, and we spent hours in the well-appointed shops stocking up with food and all kinds of little luxuries.

However, we stayed only a few days as cities are always a problem when the budget does not run to hotels, and facilities for camping cars are non-existent. The call of the rainforests grew stronger, and soon we were heading through the Ibo territories, so badly scarred by the Biafran war, towards Cameroon, Central African Republic and Zaire.

The humidity was incredible. Unlike in the desert, we were sweating simply lying in bed even before the sun came up. Our thirst was permanent, and the disgusting bottles of fruit juice on sale at roadside stalls did little to quench it.

We pulled up at yet another of these, one day, and I got out to buy a couple of the hideous brilliant orange concoctions. I returned the bottles to the stall-owner, and he called out to me as I ambled back to the car. "Hey, masa."

I strolled back to him. "Yes?"

"Dat yore woman?" he said in a conspiratorial whisper.

"Yes," I replied. "Why?"

He was staring at the seat-belt that Theresa was wearing. He leaned over to me and hoarsely confided in me. "She's strapped in." He said. 'She crazy?"

We were giving a lift to a young man from Cameroon who we'd met in Lagos and with whom we had become very friendly. He had no hope of getting back home to his mother, who was very ill, unless he could get a lift as he couldn't afford the fare. During the three days he travelled with us, he slept in a bunk which pulled out once the lift-up roof was erected, and he told us a great deal about the people and the countryside we were passing through. We enjoyed his company, and he bought us a pineapple by the roadside as a gift. It was enormous, and just out of interest I weighed it on our little scales which we used for checking the gas in our bottles. It weighed five kilos (about 11 lbs) and it had cost him the equivalent of 10 pence.

Having lived and worked in Lagos for much of his life, he could often share our amusement at some of the things we encountered along the way. One night we stopped by a small house in a clearing on the Western edge of the jungle, and asked permission to park there for the night. Having chatted to the owner of the house for a while, he came back to the van with a typically broad African grin on his face. He explained: in Cameroon, the common custom was to bury your dead in a small patch beside the house. If we wanted to go to the toilet in the night, could we please not go behind those particular bushes, as Grandma was buried just there ...

It was sad to wave goodbye to him when we finally arrived at the side of the road off to his village. But that is one of the principal aspects of overland travel: a continual making of new friends, and the inevitable parting of the ways.

As we entered the vast, steaming basin of jungle that stretched for two and a half thousand miles ahead of us we felt excited. Once out of Cameroon and into the Central African Republic, the road became more and more muddy, with large boulders liberally scattered about it, and huge troughs across it where the torrential rains had cut deep trenches in the mud.

On either side of the one-vehicle-wide track, was a thick impenetrable wall of a myriad of greens, punctuated by the occasional wild orchid or brilliant red flower. Huge arches of bamboo towered above us, making a. beautiful green ferny tunnel. Giant rust-coloured termites' nests rose up out of the ground to tower above the height of the van like sentinels along the way. And overhead, way above the tangled creepers and vines all struggling in a desperate battle for light, was a thin ribbon of sky.

For three weeks we fought our way through this gigantic greenhouse. The wooden stakes used as fences around a group of huts would sprout leaves and begin to grow as soon as they were staked into the ground. The telegraph poles (where they existed) all sprouted leaves. Lichen grew in thick clumps along the telegraph wires. Baboons and monkeys would scuttle out of the way as we trundled up to them, swiftly disappearing into the thick black undergrowth.

At night, if we were not near a small town or a Missionary station, we'd pull over to the side of the road — as far as we could — and camp alone in the forest. At first it was very scary.

Somehow, we were never alone. Not once. As soon as dusk approached and we decided to stop for the night, a small crowd of Africans would appear out of the bushes to 'see the show'. They were far more terrified of us than we were of them, and the slightest quick movement would make them start, and sometime rush into the jungle again. When we saw that they were harmless, and simply curious, we would sometimes entertain them by letting them listen to some music on a pair of headphones. Count Basie and Duke Ellington, among others, blew their minds, and one very young lad rolled his eyes in horror as he followed the stereo music from ear to ear for a while. Then he seized the 'phones and threw them down and ran off into the bushes in terror.

Once the sun had set, and we drew the curtains, the show was over till the morning. They hung around for a while, but soon became bored. Then we'd settle down in our cosy little room and try to keep cool, while the massive bugs and flying beetles bashed themselves against our windows to get to the light. Once in bed we'd lie and listen to the hissing chorus of the cicadas, and the wild and eerie screeches that echoed out of the jungle blackness. On some nights we could hear the distant pounding of drums. But never were we given any trouble by the primitive people who lived in small clearings all around us.

The absence of any form of litter struck us noticeably. Everything was precious. The children, if they were lucky enough to have one toy, would have made it out of all kinds of pieces of scrap they had found. Lids from an old tin can and blocks of wood would be assembled into the most imaginative trucks to be pushed along. The cans themselves were of course far too valuable to be given to kids, and when we gave someone an empty can which we'd finished with they were so very grateful.

I remember once, in Malawi, — a considerably more developed country — giving a small schoolboy a completely worn out inner tube. We were resting by the side of Lake Malawi, one of Africa's most beautiful and pollution-free lakes, and he rushed into the water with it and spent many happy hours splashing about with his friends and the continually-deflating tube. At the end of the day, he rolled it up the beach, and gave it back to me, thanking me very much for lending it to him.

"But I didn't lend it to you" I said. "I gave it to you. It's a present." He paused, and looked long into my eyes, perhaps to see if I was joking. Then a huge beam of happiness raced across his face. "Thank you very much," he said. "You have done a wonderful thing for me this day."

On a lesser scale, the same applied in the Congo area of the jungle. An empty one-gallon can of cooking oil brought us a gift of a huge hank of over thirty bananas. And we were the ones who were 'done'. On another occasion, we exchanged a couple of pairs of extremely ancient jeans for a beautiful solid ebony woodcarving and, again, I'm sure both parties were equally delighted with the deal.

Travelling in a mobile palace through such poverty and simplicity often made us feel hideously rich and, at times, very uncomfortable. There were other times when, with our Western (and city) conditioning, we felt distinctly nervous.

One night, in Eastern Zaire we camped for the night in a tiny clearing which, surprisingly, had no hut or other dwelling in it. We were very tired of the pressures of the jungle, and, happily, were nearly through it. As usual, a small crowd appeared out of nowhere to stand and stare at us. (We never had a night with less than eight people, and our record was forty.) I strolled over to the man I guessed was the senior guy and shook his hand. We spoke some French together, and he was obviously fairly well educated and intelligent. After a while, I told him that we were very very tired, and were sorry that we could not be as friendly as he might wish. "Oh, that's all right," he said. "We won't disturb you. This is only my family."

This was, presumably, a perfect explanation to him, and as Theresa prepared our evening meal, his large family edged their way up to and around the van to stare in at the fascinating 'goings on'. However, long before dusk had ended, the head man came up to me and told me he and his family were now going home. Perhaps he saw a flicker cross my face, and instead of reading it correctly as one of relief, he quickly reassured me. "We are going now", he said, "but we will come back after we have eaten ..."

I knew that it was completely useless to try to explain that we were exhausted from a day of battling with the boulders, and cutting our way through fallen bamboo, and fording rivers whose bridges had collapsed, and would like nothing better than to go to bed early, and read for a while. He simply wouldn't understand.

True to his word he, and three of his sons returned after an hour or so, carrying a battered home-made sort of guitar, several bottles of palm wine (an extremely potent juice made from palm fruit) and a very ancient rifle, each.

We sat around a small paraffin lamp and drank the milky coloured sweet-tasting liquid, and talked for a while. The conversation became more and more blurred, and then one of the sons started playing the guitar.

After a while, one of them got up and danced. As the flickering light of the lamp played on his shiny black dancing limbs, I smiled as I allowed my imagination to flit back to London and the life I had left so far behind. But I was nervous about the guns.

Behind me was a VW van, stuffed to the gills with all our living 'essentials' — luxuries beyond these people's wildest dreams. And they had guns, and were getting very drunk; and I had no weapon that could compete ...

They each danced in turn, and seemed to be enjoying themselves immensely. Then they cried out that it was my turn to dance. *'Oh, non!''* I said. *''Oui. Oui!''* they chorused. *''Non!''* I said. But it was useless. I knew I had to join in.

I got up and gave them a realistic, but utterly inaccurate impression of an Irish jig. Arms straight down by my side, completely expressionless face, but the most intricate footwork. (I can only do it after I've had quite a few, myself.)

They loved it. But while I was dancing, I noticed the old man turn to one of his sons, and whisper something into his ear. The son then reached over into the blackness beyond the pale amber glow of the lamplight, and drew his rifle up close beside him.

This, I thought, is it. This is our first really bad experience. And maybe our last. I finished my dance, and found I was sweating profusely. My legs felt like jelly, as it was going to be my job to protect Theresa against these four powerful men, armed with guns. How should I play it?

I remained standing, and announced that both I and Theresa were very tired. We must go to bed now, as we had a long way to go in the morning. They nodded to each other, and passed the last bottle of palm oil around. Then they all stood up, as if with a given signal.

We stared at each other for what seemed like a million years. Then the head man shot out his hand towards me. The alcohol had made my reactions slow. I looked down at it. It was extended for a handshake.

We shook hands, and they put their arms round me. We had a final swig, and then they all rolled off into the darkness and the screaming jungle noises, still singing ...

That night, as I lay in bed in the comfort of our van, I felt ashamed. Ashamed that I had brought my so-called 'civilised' attitudes with me amongst these simple, generous and friendly people. I knew now, that the father had quietly reprimanded his son for leaving perhaps his most precious possession out of sight, in the darkness, instead of keeping it close by him at all times.

Of course, I reasoned to myself, there was always the possibility that my fears might have been realised. But already I was learning that the huge majority of the people you meet in the rural areas of any country in the world have not (yet) been soured by the greed and viciousness of the city type of life. I was still carrying with me the burden of a sophisticated upbringing in a variety of cities. I wasn't learning fast enough.

I remembered how, only a few days before, I had pulled into a muddy filthy hole, laughingly called a petrol station. I'd got out and wandered round to the back of the van and chatted to the attendant as he merrily sloshed petrol into my tank — and all surrounding areas of the bodywork. "What octane is this petrol?" I enquired, mainly to make conversation, but also in the vain hope that he just *might* be able to tell me. (Petrol in many poor countries can be of appalling quality, and you constantly have to check that you're not getting a tankful of paraffin, or even water.) He stopped the pump and looked at me long and hard. "Eh?" he said.

"What *octane* is this petrol?"

"Is petrol." he said flatly.

"Yes. I know. But what OCTANE is it?"

He scratched his head, and looked around to see if help might be at hand.

It wasn't. I tried again. "Octane. Number. Do you know?"

"You want diesel?" was his reply.

I also remembered the marvellous rejoinder I got at another filling station when I pulled up beside the lone pump and was told I couldn't have any petrol. "Why not?" I asked.

"The pump. He have a mistake in him," was the reply.

What we were both beginning to learn was the fact that all over the world in both undeveloped and developed countries, the vast majority of the people are ordinary folk. Honest, simple and friendly. Whether you are passing through Gloucestershire, Tennessee, Bolivia or Tanzania it's much the same, though on very different 'levels'. There are, of course, corrupt and dishonest people everywhere too. But of the men and women that the overland traveller meets passing through their country or village, he or she is likely to encounter the violent or corrupt only in cities or in Government offices.

As we lifted up into the foothills of the East African mountains, the air was like champagne. Far behind and below us was the huge cauldron of green that had taken us three weeks to cross.

The novelty of the jungle had long since worn off. We stopped the car and got out, sucking in great lungfuls of the crisp cool air.

Down there, beneath that enormous fluffy green blanket were the scenes of all our recent battles with the roads, the rivers, the scarcity of fresh foods and even drinkable water.

The tiny towns dotted along the track had boasted shops which sold a few bales of material, tins of powdered milk, strong-smelling dried fish, monkey-meat that looked exactly like human baby, and bananas. Bananas, bananas, and more bananas. Sometimes we could get eggs, and occasionally a kind of bread. There had been little else to eat, and it was often very difficult to track down water that hadn't been carried miles by the local women in large basins on their heads — for their own consumption. Most of the rivers were slow-moving and stagnant, and we were very glad we had a water-purifier.

Far below us, too, were the primitive rafts that had ferried us over the wider rivers. Supposedly free, they would often cost us some penicillin or aspirin tablets and some cigarettes before the far bank was reached. On one occasion, I had had to remove my two batteries and take them across by canoe to the other side so that the decrepit diesel motor of a 'luxury' ferry could be started and brought over to collect our van.

The appalling roads had taken their toll on the VW too. One of the torsion-bar springs had been smashed on the boulders and ditches, and Theresa had written in our 'log' that it had been like driving over someone's vast rock garden. A perfect description. We had covered the magnificent total of 66 miles on one 8-hour day, and now we were up and out of it and heading for the Indian ocean, the big game, the tea and coffee plantations and the mountainous scenery of the east coast.

As we returned to the van, we chuckled at how, one night just before we came to the area where the pigmy tribes lived, I had sat up in bed and cried out "There's a pigmy!" in a loud clear voice, and then lay back and continued with whatever dream I was having. When we did meet them, they lived up to all the stories we'd heard about them. They were really minute, but already had lost much of their original pride and identity by the commercialisation of visiting tourists.

On the lovely smooth surface of the well-maintained mud road that headed towards the Zaire/Rwanda frontier, we passed the active volcano, 'Niragongo'. A sign said it would take only 8 hours up and five hours down, but a guide was compulsory for our protection from the wildlife.

We went into the nearby town to pick up some mail and do some shopping. Then we camped on the edge of Lake Kivu and relaxed. It is one of the two or three lakes in Africa that are free of the dreaded bug 'bilharzia' and we were able to have a long and thorough wash all over. We also cut each other's hair. Theresa took forty-five minutes to do mine. I then did hers. In twelve minutes I'd finished, and she looked into the mirror and burst into tears …

All this time, Niragongo was quietly smoking away in the distance, and we both finally agreed that we would always regret it if we didn't go up to see the red hot lava boiling in the crater.

We returned to the starting point and found out a bit more: A guide armed with an elephant gun was absolutely necessary for our protection on the lower slopes, as we could get hopelessly lost in the dense undergrowth. There was a small hut (500 feet from the top) where we would sleep the night, and then in the early hours of the morning, while it was dark, we would get the best view of the lava.

The next day we set off with 'Joseph' our guide. He carried Theresa's rucksack and I stumbled on with mine. We had a tiny petrol stove, some grub, sleeping bags and various other odds and ends.

Both of us having worked behind desks for the previous five or six years, were very unfit, and the weight of the rucksack and the steepness of the slope soon began to take its toll. We met a family of Germans who were beating a hasty retreat (with their guide) as they'd come across an enraged bull elephant thrashing about in the tangled undergrowth. No way were they going up …

We looked at Joseph, and he looked at us. He turned and continued up the slope. The elephant had disappeared, and after an hour or so we emerged out into more open terrain and started to climb in earnest.

With lungs bursting and limbs aching, we could see a small thatched hut just above us silhouetted against the sky. It hadn't been too bad, we thought. But we wouldn't like to do it three times a week for a living, like Joseph.

As we staggered up to the tiny dwelling, I turned to Joseph and panted "Is this where we sleep tonight?"

"No" he said, as he sat down on a rock and gazed out over the fertile plain below. He wasn't the most talkative guy I'd ever met in my life.

"Where do we sleep, then?" I asked.

He waved his burly black hand up towards the sky behind him and mumbled something that sounded horribly like 'the top'.

"Isn't this the top?" I said with a sinking feeling creeping slowly over me.

"No" said dear Joseph.

"How far is the top, then?" I said, not wanting to hear his answer.

"This," he said, getting up and pulling on the rucksack, "is the half-way hut. You ready?"

Psychologically, he couldn't have said anything less well timed at the moment. The second half was even worse for us, with Joseph striding ahead as if he was on a Sunday afternoon constitutional.

It was just getting dark when he finally arrived at the small octagonal pre-fabricated shelter perched precariously on the barren volcanic cone. It was freezing cold, and the wind whistled through our clothing like a knife. We collapsed into the room, unable to speak, while Joseph wandered about gathering bits of wood for a fire. Once lit, it filled the room with a choking putrid smoke, and we gulped down a bowl of hot soup and fell into our sleeping bags.

Joseph sat in front of the rusty iron stove warming his steaming feet with the firelight flickering on his shiny black face. When he thought we were asleep, he picked up one of our climbing boots and turned it over in his hands. Compared to his well-worn ordinary walking shoes, they must have seemed marvellous.

I first discovered that the hour 4.30 a.m. existed, ten thousand feet up on the top slopes of Niragongo in Zaire. I never wish to know of its existence again. Our travelling alarm shattered the silence in the hut like a fire engine bell. We staggered out of bed. Joseph was nowhere to be seen. I tried to light the petrol stove, but we'd underestimated the thing's consumption, and it ran out within a few moments.

Joseph re-appeared with the glum news that a heavy mist had come down during the night and he could see nothing over the edge of the crater. Did we want to go up the last 500 feet?

No, we didn't. But we couldn't not go, having come this far. So up we went, scrabbling over the jagged boulders. I was sick half way up, and Theresa was quietly wishing she was dead.

On the edge, the three of us sat and gazed down onto the thick white swirling mist. The sulphurous smell overwhelmed us. It was no good. Joseph said that there was little chance of it lifting, as there was no wind, and the cone sometimes stayed covered for two or three days.

Bitterly disappointed, we scrambled down to the hut, gathered up our things, and headed down to the bottom. The return journey was just as bad, as the backs of our legs were revealing muscles that we never knew were there. However, when our marvellous red van came finally into view we thanked Joseph, paid him, and threw ourselves into its warm, welcoming interior and brewed up the most delicious cup of tea ever made.

The next few weeks of our journey were incredible. We travelled on excellent well-maintained asphalt roads, through tea plantations, wild animal reserves, superb scenery, and along the magnificent coastline of Kenya and Tanzania. The sea was clear, turquoise and warm. The pale white sand, as far as the eye could see, was lined with coconut palms. We lazed, and swam, and gathered shells. We ate the most delicious fish and prawns, and one day melted into the next in a rosy euphoria. Two weeks slipped by without our moving or even noticing it. It was paradise, and we felt we deserved a rest after the many trying battles we'd fought getting ourselves and the van over the toughest roads in the world.

Finally, well refreshed, we decided to move on. There were masses of wild animals of every conceivable kind in the enormous reserves. Sometimes we had to drive very cautiously through large herds of elephant. At other times we came within a few metres of a powerful male lion. We saw buffalo, giraffe, rhinos, zebra, wildebeest, hippos, gazelles, hyenas and many many others. On one lake in Northern Kenya (Lake Nakuru) we couldn't believe our eyes: The entire circumference of the deep green water seemed to be surrounded by cherry trees in full bloom. As we approached, we realised that this pink mass was not blossom but millions and millions of flamingos. They were one of the most spectacular sights we'd ever seen, and we spent a whole day just sitting on the edge of the shallow water watching them wading about in search of food. Their pink reflections in the still green or brown water were unbelievably beautiful.

Africa was beginning to come to an end: Malawi (one of the nicest countries of all because of the particular friendliness of the people) Zambia, Rhodesia and South Africa. We relaxed with some relatives in Rhodesia for a month, and were able to learn a lot about the conflict between black and white in this part of Southern Africa. It was a pleasant time, but nevertheless we could not stomach the politics. It hurt us to see the naturally laughter-filled attitudes of the African negro supressed into a cringing 'respect' for their white masters. Compared to the repressive attitudes of the South African, the Rhodesian whites seemed more 'fatherly' and patronising, and many of them seemed genuinely to want to try to 'lift' the standard of living of the black majority onto a higher plane. But this seemed to us to be so misguided in the way it was being approached — if indeed it was a wise policy at all.

The township houses were depressing 'little boxes'. It was a manifestation of how the white man would like to think the African negro *ought* to live. Attitudes taken from the cold climates of Europe where reliability and industry are a reasonable 'norm' could not, we felt, be imposed on a sun-loving, lazy, happy-go-lucky carefree people without paying a heavy price in unhappiness and discontent.

Were it not for the politics, which we could not forget for an instant even if we'd wished to, the Southern African countries would be fabulous places in which to live. The 'garden route' along the south coast of South Africa is the richest concentration of every kind of spectacular scenery one could ever find: lakes mountains, waterfalls, gorges, sandy coves, huge miles of beach, rocky headlands, cliffs, forests, carpets of wild flowers... seemingly piled on top of each other around every corner, ending up with Cape Town, Table Mountain, and the Cape peninsula as a fitting climax.

We stayed in Cape Town and worked for twelve weeks. Theresa as a secretary, and myself as a door-to-door ball-point-pen salesman. Every morning we would emerge from our van, parked by a Youth Hostel in a wood just North of the centre, dressed in our 'smart' clothes and go off to earn the shipping money to get us to South America. It took twelve weeks to raise the total cost: (US) $1,600. (And my work permit finally came through the day before we left Africa.)

Our first continent had been a fantastic adventure. An almost continual running battle with the giant forces of nature. It was tough, and very exciting. We had certainly plunged in at the deep end for the start to our long trip, and it was the best training ground we could have had.

Ten months had already shot by since we left our home in that tiny island in Northern Europe. The van had now become our home, and had indeed proved to be ideal. It was small enough to get over the most appalling terrain or through the narrowest gaps, and yet the interior was comfortable, compact and cosy. When the pressures of the outside world were too much, we could step inside our cocoon, draw the curtains, tune into the radio, light a candle, and pour ourselves a stiff drink of whatever local brew was going. We could also escape temporarily, into our small library of paperbacks, or listen to our favourite music. Our life on the road could be remarkably civilised when we wished.

Now we were ready for what South America had to offer us. Would it be as wild as we feared it might be? Bandits and revolutions? We were about to find out as we watched the van being hoisted high into the air by a crane on the Cape Town docks. How would South Africa compare with Africa? In reminiscing mood, we mulled over our general impressions of the dark continent: Camels and Tuaregs; sand; dry parched boulders; ochres and browns; white robes; shimmering mirages; vultures; blistering heat; dry and cruel. Then there was another face of Africa: dark and mysterious; dense black-greens; butterflies and bugs; staring eyes; drooping mouths; hissing and screeching; blue-grey smoke; tangled creepers; drums; magic; dense; humid; and just a little bit frightening ... But that wasn't enough. Africa had yet another face for us: great rolling brown plains; woodsmoke smells; eucalyptus; clusters of huts; herons and hippos; spears and smiles; flat-topped trees; beads and beaches; charcoal and children; dried fish; urine; garbage; sugarcane and coloured dresses; people; always people; walking ... waiting ... And finally, in the South: flowers; beaches; wine and barbecues; 'keep-out'; winds; affluence; culture; industry; 'keep-off'; mines and machinery; litter; gardens and pets; yachts and money; church and crafts; supermarkets and scenery; privacy; 'trespassers will ...'

3.   The Americas: A clash of cultures

On December the third, I spent my birthday hanging around the Cape Town docks waiting for our most precious home-on-wheels to be hauled high in the sky on the end of a perilously fragile-looking crane wire, and lowered into the hold of the small freighter we had tracked down after endless attempts to find a ship that would take our van to South America.   Meanwhile Theresa was working as a secretary to contribute to the inflated price of crossing the South Atlantic.

Having finally arrived in Cape Town, the first task had been to track down a shipping agent that handled our sort of freight and, after very great difficulty, we found one who had a vessel coming in within the next three months.   This gave us time to find some kind of work to raise the necessary money.

I got a job selling ball-point pens on a door-to-door commission basis, and Theresa became a temporary secretary — though she had to wait several weeks to get a work permit.   (Mine actually came through on December the 2nd, but the Company I was working for didn't seem to mind too much.)

Within twelve weeks we had raised the necessary 1,600 U.S. dollars to get the van shipped and to pay for two air tickets to Buenos Aires.   We had tried to travel on the ship with the vehicle, to no avail, and this was to be the only time we failed. We also had no choice of port.   The ship was going to Argentina, and — although we had intended to arrive in Rio de Janeiro — we found it was to be Buenos Aires.   (This turned out to be a stroke of real luck, as there is no port in the world more difficult to ship a vehicle into than Rio, due to taxes and bureaucracy though nobody was aware of this in Southern Africa.)

The heart-stopping moment when the precious mobile-home was hoisted by a somewhat inadequate cable, and lowered into the hold of a freighter bound for South America. This was the first of many such moments — after a mere 11 months on the road through Africa.

Once the ship sailed, and we had made sure that the van was as thief-proof as is humanly possible, we relaxed and pottered around the beautiful Cape coastline, waiting for the flight that would overtake our little ship, and land us in Latin America to see the arrival of our van.

The transformation from English-speaking South Africa to Spanish-speaking Argentina was a shock. We took an airport bus which hurled us into the centre of Buenos Aires, and disgorged us together with our small amount of luggage to fend for ourselves.

We found a cheap hotel and, realising that we would have to share our room with a large family of wildlife — from cockroaches to mice, we moved to another one in a pleasant pedestrian street called Florida, where we stayed happily until our ship was due to arrive.

Collecting our van from the port authorities was a task we were not expecting to be particularly daunting. It was. For two and a half days we trudged from shed to shed collecting an amazing sheaf of paperwork and no less than 35 different rubber stamps on many of them. It seemed endless, and we must have covered many miles of cobbled docks before we were finally told the van was ours again.

The bonded warehouse, where we could see it parked in a dark corner, was about to close for the day. The official examinaed our papers with a fine tooth-comb. Then he announced that there was one stamp missing. We dashed off to get it, but *that* office had closed up for the day. We returned to ask if we could sleep in the van for the night, but as it was in a bonded warehouse, we couldn't. Nor would they allow us to push it outside for the night.

We had no choice but to return to the hotel for a final (we hoped) night. By mid-day the next day we were free, and on the road again.

Having spent many hours poring over maps of South America, we had decided that to cover this vast, virtually untouched-by-European-tourist chunk of land, we would head north into Brazil through Uruguay, then down to Tierra del Fuego via Buenos Aires again, and then cover the whole length of the Pacific coast and on into Central America.

Like most countries throughout the world, the inhabitants of Argentina have a basic distrust of their neighbours. This was confirmed by a resident of Buenos Aires who, on discovering to his amazement and horror that we were not planning to spend the entire time in his beloved country, but hoped to go as far as Colombia, rolled his eyes from side to side and whispered conspiratorially *"Cuidado Colombia"*. *"Porque?"* I asked. Why should I beware of Colombia?

His wordless answer spoke volumes. He simply drew his extended index finger slowly across his throat ...

First impressions of Latin America made us realise with shame how we had allowed the oppressive lifestyle in South Africa to seep into our attitudes in only three months. We found we still retained the habit of looking up before entering a doorway to check if it was for whites or blacks. We were surprised to see a negro happily walking arm-in-arm with his white girlfriend. We were suddenly aware that we had been given back a freedom that is unknown in southern Africa, and which we were not fully aware we had lost in such a short time.

With a full tank of (then) relatively cheap Argentine petrol, plus our spare tank brimming over as well, we hoped we might get through Uruguay without having to pay their horrific fuel prices. This scheme worked, and as we entered Brazil we were down to our last few litres.

Crossing into or out of Brazil by road is easy, unlike shipping in, so we were soon on our way looking out for the first filling station. We ran out of fuel, and cursed our meanness in not lashing out on even a few paltry litres at the Uruguayan border.

A VW beetle stopped and offered assistance. He drained a couple of bottles-full from his tank and told us there was a gas-station only 5 miles along the road.

When we pulled in we discovered that their 'Super' had run out, and they only had 'Regoolar'. OK, we thought. Our VW used Regular in Britain (minimum 91 Octane) so even if it was a bit rough, it would get us to Porto Allegre — the next big city — where we could top up with better quality stuff.

What we were unaware of was that Brazilian regular is only 67 octane, and the specially designed local VW (and other) engines, have concave pistons to take this into account ...

It was only a couple of hundred kilometres down the road, on Christmas day, that our engine seemed to explode, and we came to a grinding halt at the side of the road.

The little black cloud of gloom that had settled over us was partly dispersed by the arrival of an unbelievably decrepit van bulging with children. Did we need any help they enquired somewhat unnecessarily in their fluent Portuguese which was vaguely possible to interpret by sign-language.

It was agreed that we be towed to the main VW dealers in Porto Allegre where, having thanked the family profusely, we sat down and cooked our first Christmas dinner on the road; boiled eggs and toast. It was not a happy time.

Fortunately for us, Christmas is not celebrated in most parts of the world with the enthusiasm of the Europeans. Consequently, the Brazilians were back at work on Boxing Day, and we had high hopes of being on the road again very rapidly.

Our engine was made in Germany, and as the second largest VW factory is in Brazil, we learned that almost every part was of different design, and few European spares were available.

The only solution to the damaged pistons and valves was a rebore, we were told. So, it had to be.

Four days and nights later, we emerged from that hell-hole with four Ford pistons, Mercedes valves, the distributor 180° out of alignment, and countless other trivial little incongruities such as spark-plug leads crossed ...

It was amazing that the engine ran at all, but unaware of all this, we were treated to a delightful concert by the garage mechanics, and were then waved on our way.

This was the beginning of a string of troubles too tedious to mention in any detail. To summarize them, we had to have our engine removed (never less than two full days work) and put back (usually another full day's work) no less than seven further times. Each time we were assured that the particular problem was now definitely cured. And each time the trail of oil or the gross misfiring that developed proved that all was by no means well.

The real problem was that our European-style engine was too complicated for third-world mechanics — even authorised dealers — and we would have been considerably better off had we been travelling in the simple 1600 cc engined vehicle that they all knew so well. However, having read several books on driving in the Andes, I had erroneously assumed that we would need all the power we could get just to get up to those dizzy heights. It was not so, as we were to find out.

The Eastern side of South America is in general not unlike many parts of Latin Europe. The richer countries lie on this side, with Brazil and Argentina competing fiercely for industrial status. Whereas the Brazilians are fiery and temperamental, with a tremendous zest for life, their southern neighbours in Argentina (and to a certain extent in Uruguay) are somewhat more sophisticated and gentle in their approach to life. From a distinctly male point of view, I have never seen so many superbly beautiful women as in the centre of Buenos Aires, and yet, in Brazil, there are something like five females to every male, and with that sort of competition, the country is a male paradise as well.

Having seen Cape Town, I was sure that there could be no more lovely setting for a city. I had felt the same about the mind-blowing beauty of the Victoria Falls. Both of these were sights that I was certain could not be surpassed. I was wrong on both counts.

Rio de Janeiro is the jewel in the navel of the world. It is utterly magic — nestling beneath the 2,000 foot-high craggy mountains that drop sheer into the dazzling blue ocean, fringed with the glimmering white beaches that continue for 8,000 miles of Brazilian coastline. As if this were not enough, add the velvet green forests, the small clusters of coastal lakes, and the glistening white blocks of flats that hug the coast, and it makes a jig-saw of visual excitement that cannot be bettered.

However, once you come down from the great heights of the mountain-tops above the city, you take your life in your hands as you endeavour to compete with the inhabitants of this frenetic city as they hurl themselves and their mechanical coffins from place to place.

Brazil has the worst road-death statistics in the world. And to experience Brazilian driving is to leave you in no doubt whatsoever that they're justified in this dubious record. Theresa spent more time either on the floor of the driving cab, quivering like a jelly, or in tears of terror than she did anywhere else in the world.

On one occasion (on the coastal road between Porto Allegre and Rio) we were grinding up a long hill with sheer mountain above us to the left, and a sheer drop to the sea on the right. The road was three lanes wide, and unfenced on the ocean side. A huge truck began to overtake us as we approached the blind top of the hill and, to my horror, another one started to overtake the two of us at the same time. So, as we headed towards the top of the hill, the three of us were occupying all available lanes in a row, leaving no space whatsoever for the inevitable oncoming traffic.

Craven cowards that we were, we pulled in and stopped.

Between Porto Allegre and Rio, we'd seen a city marked on the map, and had decided to have our first bunch of mail sent there. It looked like a medium-sized place, thereby making the collection less of a hassle than in a big city such as Rio... That's what we reckoned...

The city was Sao Paulo. We'd never heard of it. But we'll never forget it.

As we belted along the multi-lane freeway signed Sao Paulo, we could see the suburban swelling on the horizon. The haze of pollution drew nearer as we vainly tried to keep our careering van at a safe speed (flat out, and apparently almost stationary compared to the remaining flow of traffic).

The overhead signs flashed past as we soared up onto a massive elevated section. They depicted suburban areas with incomprehensible names that meant nothing to us. We waited for the inevitable 'CENTRO' sign. It didn't come. We travelled on. Still no 'CENTRO' indicating at least we were half way through this infernal ocean of thronging houses and factories.

Suddenly, we were spewed out on the far side of the city, and on the race track to Rio. There seemed to be no way in which we could return, and we were sucked along Northwards until we realised that our mail would have to remain there until we returned — if we dared.

Thirteen million people lived in Sao Paulo when we flew over its rooftops in our van, and it seemed as though they were all on the highway to Rio, bent on suicide on that day.

We did in fact return, and eventually found the main Post Office where we battled to collect a tiny portion of the mail which we knew had been sent there. What letters we did manage to extract from the unbelievable chaos were a joy, and made up for the ones that are still probably gathering dust in the overflowing pigeon-holes of mis-filed correspondence.

Compared to the animation of Rio, the new capital, Brasilia was a sterile desert of indulgence by the group of architects who had overseen the creation of this ultra-new city in the centre of a wild bushy plain. They had had to fly in the first bricks until the long flat road was built, and there had also been the need to construct an artificial lake to cater for the city's needs.

The buildings were shoddily made, revealing huge cracks in the concrete even before they were finished. The architecture was interesting in a style of the '50s, but little consideration seemed to have been given to the fact that this place was to be inhabited by and therefore the servant of, real, living, two-legged human beings. We were told that on Friday nights, the dash to the airport by people wanting to enjoy a more lively weekend in the crowded, jostling, but alive atmosphere of their beloved capital-that-was had to be seen to be believed.

Before we left Brazil, we visited the most spectacular waterfalls in the world. Not half as well-known as the Victoria falls, the Iguassu Falls tumble out of the Argentine rain-forest presenting an unparalleled spectacle to the Brazilians on the frontier between the two countries. Millions of gallons per hour crash over the precipice in the shape of an inverted 'Y' and, on the Argentine side you can walk along the top of the falls for about 5 kilometers through the dappled green rain-drenched trees inhabited by the most brilliantly coloured enormous butterflies and tropical parrots.

On the Brazilian side, the canopy of green frames the surging thundering wall of sparkling white foam as it crashes down into the boiling cauldron of spray and jagged black rocks below. We were both rendered speechless by its sheer beauty as we watched the sun rise into the pale eggshell blue sky above this constantly surging display of such immense but delicate power.

Having returned to Buenos Aires, where we explored the City more thoroughly, we set off on the long route down to the most southerly town in the world; Ushuaia, on the island of Tierra del Fuego.

At that time, most of the southern part of the road was unpaved, and covered with small sharp stones which flew up in a lethal spray whenever an oncoming vehicle shot past. They also cut our already-nearly-bald tyres to ribbons, and we averaged 1½ punctures a day for ten days of long hard driving through some of the most tediously boring scenery we ever encountered.

The absolute flatness of the Pampas grasslands is shatteringly dull, and we found ourselves getting really excited when we came across a two-foot-high bush that broke up the wind-swept monotony of this part of our journey.

Eventually we came to the tiny ferry that was to carry us onto the island of Tierra del Fuego. It was high and dry, with the edge of the sea a good 400 metres away. Yet within a couple of hours, the massive tide had floated it and we were on our way again.

From Tierra del Fuego, the best part of South America was about to begin. It had been a long haul just to get down there, and were we to do a journey again, we would skip Patagonia altogether thereby saving the enormous mileage for the relatively few highlights.

However, as soon as we started northwards, the excitement of travelling in this part of the world began to increase. Our first taste was the glacier Moreno on Lake Argentino. This massive constantly moving wall of ice, with its brilliant deep blue shadows, ends in a 70 ft high cliff which continually 'calves' gigantic blocks of ice which crash down into the steely grey lakewater below. On the top, as you look down from a nearby hilltop, it looks like a giant cake with frosty icing, and the ceaseless rumbling and cracking of the ice sounds like an unending firework display.

We sat in the gentle sunlight and watched the display for a day and a half, taking bets on which precariously balanced ten-ton chunk would be the next to break away and roar down into the lake, causing a massive wave of water to fan out from the newly-born iceberg.

The first (of several) times we crossed the Andes was in the South, where they are rolling and relatively gentle. It was a memorable drive, in that our van was towed by a powerful mercedes saloon driven by a dead German. The clutch on the VW had gone, and we needed to get to Chile where (unlike Argentine) VW were comprehensively represented. I steered the van while Theresa sat in the car and talked with and listened to the dead German. He wasn't of course so dead that his heart had stopped beating and had gone cold, he was simply *officially* dead. Having crashed his plane during the last war, he decided he'd had enough of that kind of game, and stayed put (alive and well) until it was all over and he'd lost. Then he wended his way

One of the mountain pass roads over the Andes. This one, by no means the highest, went to 12,000 ft. between Santiago (Chile) and Mendoza (Argentina)

back to The Fatherland only to discover that his wife, having been informed by the German Government of the day that her hubby was missing presumed dead, had been happy to accept not only a fat pension but a new man in her life.

Faced with the sudden re-appearance of husband No 1, it had generally been agreed that to give up the pension and all that went with her new lifestyle was not the most appealing of ideas, so our gallant first husband promptly returned to the metaphorical grave he'd found so comfortable in South America, and remained well and truly dead.

For a corpse, he certainly drove a Mercedes pretty well, and entertained Theresa with war-stories similar to those she'd heard from her father — but from the other point of view.

And so it was that we entered Chile for the first time. Limping but proud, we were taken to the VW dealers who gave us a Volvo clutch, and took days to put it in. We passed the time waiting for some money to arrive being lavishly entertained by the local Bank manager and his family, and learning a great deal about the real truth of the political situation in Chile both before and after the demise of Allende and his government.

The more we travelled and met people in Chile, and the more we talked to all classes and types of local inhabitants, the more we realised that what we were hearing on the BBC World Service and reading in what European or American papers and magazines we could find was diametrically opposed to what we (and all the other overlanders we were meeting) were learning from the ordinary people in both cities and the country.

Our affinity with the Latin American people was beginning to flourish as we learned to speak tolerable Spanish and therefore comprehend some of their previously incomprehensible gestures and habits. Certainly we found the Southern Argentinians (including the inhabitants of a Welsh-speaking village!) and the Southern Chileans to be among the most hospitable of our whole journey.

Chile divides naturally into three geographical areas: The south comprises a myriad of lakes and volcanoes, with gentle misty rolling scenery that should not be missed. The central strip is less agricultural and more industrial. Highly populated by comparison, it contains several large cities including the capital, Santiago, while to the North, the remainder of the Country is arrid, barren desert bordered on the East by the snow-capped peaks of the Andes, and on the West by the Pacific coastline, dotted with small fishing villages and ports.

48

From Santiago we had planned to travel North through Argentina, so we crossed the Andes via a spectacularly high pass and down to a town called Mendoza. However, on arriving there we discovered that during the short time we had been in Chile, the price of petrol had tripled, so we shot back over the pass and continued North through the Atacama desert.

The road was paved and the journey easy. It was a totally different kind of desert to the Sahara, and we would occasionally deviate to visit the coastal ports where the sardine industry flourished despite the strenuous efforts of the thousands of pelicans and other sea birds.

The real highlight of this fascinating part of the world, however, turned out to be Peru, Bolivia, Ecuador and Colombia, and we realised how fortunate we had been to have had the previous months travelling through the rest of the sub-continent to acclimatise ourselves to the Latin way of life, and to familiarise ourselves with the language, and all its idiosyncrasies.

The phrase *'No hay'* — pronounced *'No eye'* — is firmly engraved on the hearts of every overlander who travels in South America. Literally translated, it means 'there isn't' and implies 'I don't know (or care)'. However, it is used with a frequency that is guaranteed to start you screaming with frustration within seconds.

For example, you're driving through a town in search of the centre. You call out to a local *"Donde es el Centro?"* assuming that he can point you (even vaguely) in the direction of the centre.

His reply? Inevitably: *"No hay!"*

You go to a market to buy some food. There are stalls and stalls of marvellous fresh vegetables, including mountains of tomatoes. You want to know how much they cost. *"Buenas dias"* you say, in your cheery Spanglish, *"Cuanta questa los tomates?"*

The reply? Inevitably: *"No hay"*

You try again, pointing at them. *"Los tomates, cuanta questa un kilo?"* And still it comes: *"No hay"* and no one can explain why you should be denied the luscious fruits except that, being a 'gringo' you are not an acceptable customer.

Another aspect of South American travel that drives you to despair is the proliferation of checkpoints. Presumably they give employment to the bored military, but they frustrate the tourist beyond measure. They're worst in Bolivia, where on one day we passed through no less than fifteen of the bloody things.

They are usually a small hut with a pole across the road, and a snoozing soldier sitting on a battered chair with a gun in his lap. As you approach, he opens one eye and, on seeing a foreign number-plate, promptly closes it again. You draw up and are immediately engulfed in the cloud of dust you've been staying ahead of as your rear wheels churn up the fine talcum powder surface of the parched roads.

Staggering out of the fog, you approach the hut clutching your passport. Inside the door, in the inky blackness of the usually windowless room the elaborate performance begins: in a massive book, across two large pages, you enter every conceivable detail about you, your wife/girl-friend, your family, the colour of your father's eyes, your place of birth, the last address you lived at, the next address you're going to, your aunts, your uncles, your vehicle details, the money you have, and on and on and on. If you are lucky, you can fill it out yourself and be on your way within 20 minutes. If not, the details are written at a speed equivalent to carving the letters in granite, and you are there for an age.

Formalities completed, you can go, only to encounter another of the hideous things within half an hour of driving along a road without a single junction and therefore rendering the second checkpoint a mere carbon copy of the previous one.

It was amusing to see the entries in the books where travellers were allowed to write the details themselves:

'Ludwig van Beethoven, who's father's eyes were red, was travelling from Delhi to Alcatraz in a pram; and he was accompanied by Florence Nightingale who was born in Belgrade zoo in 1995, and whose address was the White House, Washington. It certainly lightened the tedium, and must have puzzled the inspectors if ever they bothered to read the pages of entries.

Nevertheless, Bolivia was a delightful country, and the people were considerably more friendly than the Peruvians who seemed to be somewhat spoiled by the increasing number of tourists visiting the Inca graveyards, and the various 'sights' such as Machu Picchu — the lost city of the Incas.

This is one of the worst stretches of road on the North side of Lake Titicaca in Bolivia. It was necessary to 're-arrange' the boulders in the road before the minivan could pass without grounding on the dried-up river bed.

To get there, there's a choice of two trains; The tourist one, and the local one. The latter is infinitely more fun. Packed with locals it rumbles its uncomfortable way along the side of a river, through incredibly high peaks between a tiny village called Ollantaitambo (the furthest point one is able to take a vehicle) and the base of the mountain on top of which the lost city is truly lost — apart from the air.

A small group of overlanders gathered at Ollantaitambo on the evening before we planned to go, and when the train steamed in to the station we scrambled aboard and eventually found what are laughingly called seats. I was sitting next to an American overlander with a crazy Afro hairstyle and the inevitable poncho. The local family couldn't take their eyes off him and eventually the father struck up the courage to ask him the frustratingly-frequent conversation opener *'De donde esta ustede?''* (Where are you from?)

Chris. the American gringo, answered somewhat grumpily *"La Luna''* (The Moon). This caused a complete silence from the surrounding passengers, who had settled down to be entertained by the forthcoming conversation between the father of the family and this strange-looking gringo. No-one spoke as the train rattled on through the valleys. The embarrassed silence became increasingly apparent. Chris looked at the man, and the man looked at Chris. Nobody knew what to do or say. Eventually Chris, realising that he had, perhaps, been a trifle rude, decided to break the ice and re-open the conversation by enquiring where they, the family, came from.

"De donde estas ustedes?''

There was a momentary pause while they stared at each other, and then, with a delightful twinkle, the father replied *"Mars''.*

The lost city of the Incas is not one of the most exceptional of the welter of ruins in Peru. However its situation is formidably beautiful. The peak on which the city's ruins were discovered only 60-odd years ago is almost sheer to the river valley that surrounds it on three sides 2,000 feet below. Then like the sides of a gigantic bowl, the mountains rise up again on all sides like walls of stone, lightly covered with blue-green vegetation. To photograph its beauty is impossible, and usually all one sees is the peak of the central mountain on which the ruined city rests.

For many weeks, as we explored the Andean villages and towns in Peru and Bolivia, we stayed at an average of 12,000 feet which was the limit of our little altimeter. On one occasion we drove up to 15,000 ft it went berserk! Then, suddenly, we would find we were down to a paltry 8,000 feet.

Had we had a truck and somewhat more money, we could have filled it in a day at just one of the multitude of local markets selling every kind of craft and weaving. By comparison with what we were used to back home, the prices were staggeringly cheap, even for precious metals such as silver, or gemstones such as turquoise.

I bought a lump of natural unpolished turquoise for the inflated price of six U.S. dollars. Once back home I was interested to get an offer of £50 from a rock shop...

The days and weeks rolled by as we wandered through the Andean roads, sometimes taking a full day to reach a point we had been able to see when we set off in the morning. The hair-pin bends were so prolific that by the end of a four-hour spell of driving, my arms would be aching from manipulating the steering wheel.

In Ecuador we encountered the amazing tribe 'Los Colorados de Santo Domingo' who dye their hair with a thick sticky bright red paste and cut it in a pudding basin style (*see photograph on* page 55). They wear very little clothing and, reputedly, drink paraffin to clean out their insides. (Happily, they don't smoke).

In Colombia we were subjected to a minor earthquake while accepting drinks from a German family who lived on the 8th floor of a block of flats. As we entered their apartment, and noticed the pictures on the walls swinging back and forth and the central light fitting swaying gently in the apparent lack of breeze, I thought it couldn't be the drink as we hadn't even been offered one yet.

"Oh look" said out hostess standing by the window and watching the lights of the entire city below flickering on and off like some Christmas display, "we're having a tremor".

I didn't see the humour, as the gathering laughed and poured out the drinks. I just wondered, as I pretended not to clutch the nearest table, whether they'd noticed the castanet-like noise of my teeth chattering and my knees knocking. Apparently they hadn't, and very rapidly I was able to assure myself that my apparently failing leg muscles were entirely due to German hospitality. It was good to get back to ground level and the comparative comfort of our van.

Browsing through the detailed log which we kept of our journey, it is interesting to note how we settled into the nomadic life we had become used to since we left London nearly eighteen months previously. I quote from the entry of 4/5 July (an average entry): "Off to Saquisili market, but first a lot more climbing to do. Lovely wild flowers and thick bushes gave way to pampas and llamas when we reached 12,000 ft. Market not very good. Only found 3 of the 7 plazas. A few stalls with ponchos and tapices but nothing much else. Tried for ages to barter our omelette pan and a bath towel for a poncho but they wouldn't... they wanted MORE! Returned to Quito, and bought a shrunken head which we posted to (nephew) Tim."

I cannot claim that the head was in fact genuinely human like the ones we saw in the museums, though if it was an imitation, it was staggeringly realistic, and resulted in a vitriolic letter from home several months later when it had been placed between the sheets of the bed allocated to an elderly visiting relative.

Having spent enough time in East Africa to lull us into the false belief that we could cope with local thieves in any part of the world, we realised that we were only apprentices in the game. In Colombia, thieving is a National Sport.

Nothing removable is left on the exterior of any vehicle — even the indigenous ones. Consequently one never sees hub-caps, wing-mirrors or wipers on any car. When it rains, the entire city of Bogota grinds to a temporary halt while people unlock their glove compartments, and attach their hidden wipers for as long as it is raining. When it stops, the performance is reversed.

One of the officially-recognised dodges is the snatching of ear-rings, glasses and of course, handbags and cameras. Being a country where they drive on the left of the road — in common with the whole of South America — the drivers became tired of having their watches snatched off their wrists as they lolled their elbows over the windows in traffic jams.

They devised a seemingly foolproof way around this problem by wearing their watches on their *right* wrists — well into the interior safety of the vehicle.

However, this worked for only a short time, as the unbelievably enterprising thieves came up with a counter move: They'd wander up to the watchless left wrist happily lolling over the door window, and stub the butt of a lit cigarette onto it. With a

Los Colorados de Santo Domingo, Ecuador. The curious 'hat' is in fact his hair, plastered in thick bright red paste and cut in true pudding-basin style. The Colorado (red people) tribe are reputed to drink paraffin — though happily they do not smoke! There also appears to be a distinct shortage of Wellington boots.

yell of pain, the unhappy driver would then clasp his aching hand with the other one and bingo! the watch would be ripped off.

You think I'm exaggerating? I'm not. This is the land where a VW bus of overlanders had their entire roof-rack emptied *as they drove along* — wondering why the truck overtaking them was passing them so slowly. This is the land where two land-rover travellers found *their* roofrack had been emptied while they sat inside in the rain studying a road map. This is the land where one of you stays with the vehicle while the other goes into the gold museum, or to buy some food — *or else!*

Nevertheless, the Colombians are delightful rogues who at least give you a generous smile as they rip you off.

As for bandits, we don't believe we ever saw one, and certainly never had anything other than the utmost courtesy from the often wild-looking mountain people. However, we weren't foolish enough to risk parking for the night in totally isolated spots.

Suddenly South America was over, and we were on the 17-hour ferry from Cartagena to Panama — a more expensive (per mile) journey than even the Dover—Calais route.

After the incredible spectacle of South America, we had to admit that Central America was somewhat tame by comparison. However the travellers we met heading South were quietly blowing their minds at the scenery, the ruins, the customs, the people — and of course the inevitable bureaucracy, so we kept quiet. What particularly amused us was the North Americans moaning about the appallingly bad Mexican dirt roads. To us they were bliss. Regularly graded, wide and smooth, they were seemingly as good as tarmac, though to someone used to Interstate Highways, they must have seemed a bit rough...

Once we had paused to overhaul both exterior and interior of the van, in the safety and comfort of the US Canal zone on the Panama Canal, we flashed through the battery of tiny Central American Countries at a rate of knots. It seemed that one had barely passed through one border when the frontier at the other side was looming on the horizon.

For us, Guatemala was particularly fascinating, for both the colourful clothes and the extremely well-stocked markets. A trip off the main Pan American Highway to the ancient ruins of Tikal was a special highlight that shouldn't be missed by any overlander — regardless of the dire tales circulating about the state of the roads in that area.

A dramatic stretch of jungle road in the rain forests of central America. Although sometimes very difficult to negotiate, this one led to the startling complex of ruined pyramids at Tikal in Guatemala — and was well worth the effort.

We became totally ruin-happy on the Yucatan peninsula. Stopping only at a small proportion of them, we nevertheless never wanted to see another ruin again by the time we left the peninsula.

After a sojourn in Mexico City, and several visits to the Anthropological Museum, the call of the mighty U.S.A. became so strong, we had to say farewell to Latin America, and head for the frontier and the 13th largest city in the U.S.A: San Antonio.

Within a mere few hundred metres of no-man's-land at the border between Mexico and the U.S.A., there is a change of life-styles so dramatic that it took our breath away. The two cultures don't clash gently, they collide with dramatic force.

During the past 18 months, the two of us had passed through 18 African Countries, and 17 Latin American ones of which barely a handful were what Europeans would call 'developed'. We had met local people who were delighted to be given a gift of an empty can and who marvelled at the sight of a mirror.

We had seen poverty on an unbelievable scale, and we had also encountered a warmth and generosity that seems to be the characteristic of those who have little or nothing.

Now, at last we were entering the most powerful nation in the world...

During our stay in Mexico City we had met a well-travelled North American who was able to relate his Country to many other parts of the world, so we peppered him with questions about the U.S.A. and asked him to give us a route that would cover all the main aspects of his vast country.

The route he gave us, he said, would give us the best possible impression of the States and Canada, taking into account the seasons etc.

It was the 18th of September when we crossed the frontier, and we had allocated approximately 6 months in which to travel around North America. The route we took was designed to cover the five principal areas of the US:
1) Texas (unique unto itself)
2) The deep South
3) The Eastern Seaboard — including New York, New England and the fall colours
4) The Mid-West — the breadbasket of the U.S.
5) The West Coast

One of a multitude of ancient Mexican statuettes to be seen in the Anthropological Museum in Mexico City. A superb museum and well worth the six hours we spent absorbed by its well placed displays.

Adding Canada — and particularly the wild countryside on the north side of the Great Lakes, we were assured by our friend that we would have a true picture of this vast sub-continent.

In all, we covered 11,000 miles in the six months, and I believe we could not have had better advice on our route.

Within a few hours we had our first shock: A Texan 'comfort-station'. It was a small lay-by on the side of the immaculate highway where we could rest up for the night. Twice a day a team of men came to clean it and polish it until it gleamed. There was toilet paper in the toilets (sorry, 'rest-rooms'). There were seat-shaped paper covers to put on the seats for added hygiene. The grass looked as if it had been cut with nail-scissors, and there were showers for the weary traveller. And what's more, it was FREE.

This was just the start. As we moved on we were constantly faced with a lifestyle that was more like a piece of futuristic science-fiction. The orderliness; the supermarkets; the sign-boards; flashing signs; and the wealth.

On the plus side, the U.S.A. is exceptionally beautiful, and the inhabitants treasure their natural beauty. There was virtually no litter — compared to the mountains of it in countries like Peru. The cost of living was cheap — in comparison to the wealth of products in those gigantic drive-in supermarkets. The colours of the maple trees in New England in the Fall was utterly breathtaking, and the sight that impressed us more than any other, anywhere in the world, was the Grand Canyon. No amount of the usual 'oversell' of roadside billboards could destroy this loveliest and most magnificent of sights. Scenically, the U.S.A. is far more exciting than we had thought possible. States such as Utah, Oregon, Alabama and upstate New York seem to be unjustifiably overshadowed by the attractions of New York City, Los Angeles, Chicago or Dallas.

Particular highlights for us included a visit to a NASA research station, a carnival in New Orleans — though the prostitution of the old jazz French Quarter to the tourist industry was a great disappointment. We loved New York City, and were bowled over by the vibrant museum of Modern Art. Our favourite city was San Francisco, but it was always the natural beauty that appealed to us most.

On the critical side, we found the fast food appalling; the sheer grossness of such overall wealth disgusting; the insularity of the vast majority of the people horrifying; and the general ignorance about things that weren't directly related to the U.S. or the dollar quite terrifying.

One of the joys of overlanding is that with the vehicle serving as a people-magnet, you meet and talk to a continuous flow of curious minds. The questions are sometimes infuriatingly repetitive: 'Where are you from? What is your name?' etc. Nevertheless they demonstrate an innate curiosity about visitors and foreigners that shows an awareness of the outside world — however ignorant.

In the US that curiosity seems to have been killed. People are private. Heads turn the other way rather than intrude and risk being shunned. Wealth, security and comfort seem to deaden the mind in many so-called developed nations around the world. If an approach is made to a foreigner, it frequently tends to be a 'formula' approach on the lines of those hideously commercial clichés like "Have a nice day" accompanied by a mechanical grin.

The East and West coasts tend to be considerably more cosmopolitan and internationally-minded than the huge central areas from Virginia to Colorado. In these vast central areas, the nearest foreigners are the Canadians ('Well they're almost the same as us, aren't they?') and the Mexicans in the South ('and we don't really want to have much to do with them and their funny foreign language, do we?') so perhaps one cannot blame the mid-west Americans for being so out of touch with the rest of the world. The world, for them, IS the U.S.A.

I recall pulling into a gas station near Kansas one day and, to my surprise, seeing a fellow motorist who had been staring at my British Number-plates, overcome by his curiosity, strolling towards me. "Hi" he said.

"Hi"

"Which State 're you from?"

I noted the fact that the possibility of my number-plates being those of a different country had not even occurred to him and replied: "I'm from London, England."
"'re those British plates?" he enquired.
"Yes"

"Did you ship it over here?"

"Well not exactly. We drove it down through Africa, and then shipped to Argentina, and then drove it up here through Central America and into Texas."

"Wow! Gee! You sure must've seen some sights on a trip like that!" he exclaimed. "Jeez!"

"Yes, we sure did" I added. We..."

"Have you seen the Eisenhower Memorial, down the road?"

The United States and Canada are places for holidays. They're not really 'overlander' territories. Everything is carefully mapped, and facilities for the foreign visitor abound. For that reason, although we had some pleasant and comfortable times, and enjoyed the multitude of luxuries such as a warm coin-operated laundromats in places such as Thunder Bay (on the North of Lake Superior) when the thermometer dropped to minus 23°C, we were not really adventuring. It was all too easy and organised. The challenge had gone out of our travelling and we began to long for our own personal adventures on the road.

And so, when the day came and we were on the freighter from San Francisco to Japan, we were suddenly rejuvenated, and eager for what lay ahead again. And we were right.

Just one of many freezing nights on the road. Here, in Salt Lake City in the USA, the weight of the snow made the lift-up roof sag during the night. The next morning, it took 4 hours before all the ice had melted - on the inside of the van.

4. The East, Japan, India, and home.

"What do you do for a living?" I enquired of the inscrutably bland face opposite me. He was sitting cross-legged on a tatami mat in his house, and his wife had poured us some scented Japanese tea. I was trying to combine being comfortable and sitting with my legs crossed under me.

"Lentils" came his reply.

"Do you mean vegetables?" I asked, somewhat puzzled. His English was poor, but I had been told by a charming VW agent in the heart of Tokyo that this friend of his might allow us to park our van in his small but adequate back yard for a few weeks while we tried to earn some shipping money by teaching English conversation.

He looked puzzled at my question. His answer told me little more. "Lag Lentils" he said.

In fact, I wasn't particularly fascinated by what he did for a living, but in this situation of mutual assessment, I was doing my bit in making polite conversation.

"Lag lentils?" I enquired. "What are they?"

"For creaning and porishing" he said, without a flicker of expression. I knew I was getting in deeper, but I blundered on. After all, I had only just arrived in Japan, and couldn't be expected to understand all their customs and traditions in a few days.

He saw my bewilderment, and came to my rescue — embarrassed that his English was so poor.

"Lags" he said again, ever so slightly louder. "Lags - for creaning". And as he stressed his last word, he made a horizontal circular movement with one clenched hand, and my desperate brain latched onto the miracles of interpretive sign language. "Aaaaaah!" I cried. "RAGS! Rag rentals!"

He smiled. No, he beamed. "You are in the business of renting out rags for cleaning and polishing" I said.

"Yes." he said. "Lag lentils".

During our time in Japan, we came across a hilarious collection of misuses of the 'Engrish' language. One man 'corrected' butterfries'. And when we asked if he minded killing such beautiful creatures for his collection, were told 'Yes. But it satisfies the maniac in me'.

It took us six full days to hunt out, somewhere in the crowded city of Tokyo, where we could park the VW for longer than a day or two. On the sixth day we found a convent with a small field. It was run by Australian nuns and Canadian monks, and for a small consideration towards convent funds, we could stay for as long as we (reasonably) liked. It was a marvellous spot to camp, and each day we would leave the van dressed in adequately smart clothes to take our evening classes in English conversation.

During the day, we passed the time writing stories and exercises for the language school, so within only 12 weeks we had earned 4,000 US dollars and had enough to bring us back into the black from the exceptionally costly trans-pacific freight charge, plus the estimated cost of the freighters to India when we were ready to go.

We had decided that due to the cost of shipping, we would omit Australia from our itinerary for a number of other reasons as well as the purely financial one.

It was a difficult decision, as it meant missing out on one of the planet's complete continents. But then what would we gain if we went there? We discussed the question at great length with some Australians and a German couple who had travelled virtually everywhere we had — including Australia. They held opinions we valued and trusted, and the overriding points were these: Australia has nothing scenically to compare with the terrain we had already passed through in Africa and South America. Their desert, by comparison with the Sahara is a very poor relation. Their mountains and other scenic beauties can in no way compare with the Andes or the foothills of the Himalayas. Lakes? Volcanoes? Ancient cultures? Wildlife?

Inevitably, there was little to pull us into another expensive shipping in order to visit a basically English-speaking lifestyle in an unspectacularly vast land. We simply couldn't reconcile the trip just to include kangaroos, the Great Barrier Reef, Ayers Rock, koalas, the Sydney Harbour bridge & opera house, and Holden cars, when compared with totally foreign and endlessly fascinating cultures such as the one we had just found ourselves immersed in at the moment. And so, we stayed 5 months in Japan, and loved every minute of it.

Of all the countries we visited on our trip, they all, with one exception, could be somehow related to our lifestyle back home. Many were very different, but they nevertheless had some affinity with what we had experienced both home and abroad That one exception was Japan.

Here we came up against an impenetrable wall of alienation to the standards we had experienced all over the world. By teaching for twelve weeks, we crossed some of the frontiers that the Japanese erect between their own and the 'gaijeen' (round-eye foreigner).

We were treated as 'sensai' or 'masters' and were given a respect that is not afforded the ordinary Western tourist. We were not viewed as gigantic children, incapable of understanding the sophisticated adult Japanese ways. Instead, by asking our class to talk about (say) marriage or religion, we were treated — somewhat stumblingly — to a series of discourses on arranged marriages, and the subtle differences between Zen Buddhism and the Shinto religion. We enjoyed insights into *why* the employing Company was more important than the family, and how such an incredibly honest and polite people could have been swept into a situation where they committed such outrages during the war.

However, we also discovered the truth in the old adage that the more you learn, the more you realise you've yet to learn. But of the little we did absorb, we discovered a people with whom we could have happily spent the rest of our lives. The propaganda that we had seen on British TV about desperately overcrowded smog-filled streets is a drastic distortion of the truth. Japan is predominantly forested. It's a green and beautiful land, with occasional brilliant flashes of orange temples nestling in the shady woodlands. The people are shy, polite, intrinsically honest, charming, elegant and extremely sophisticated.

Virtually everything they touch — from the food on your plate to a corner of a petrol station forecourt — is tinged with the seemingly inherent sense of design that is such a strong characteristic of this island people.

They love their ceremonies, and there's a festival in the streets of a Japanese town or city every week of the year. They adore children, and treat them with an indulgence that is difficult to understand when one watches them creating havoc in a huge department store. There is little poverty in this highly organised society, and yet some of their customs and traditions seem positively mediaeval side by side with the miraculously efficient modern public services.

Our main grouse with the Japanese was the apparent lack of any kind of individualism. After some weeks in their land, we ached to see one beard, coloured shirt, or jay-walker. Even on a deserted evening street, there would be the inevitable huddle of locals waiting to cross the traffic-free road only when the little green man lit up.

Unfortunately, most visitors to Japan hop from Tokyo (if they leave there at all) to Kyoto, and maybe one or two other cities before flying home. The joy of travelling about the country under one's own steam and discovering remote villages and fishing communities is the only way to discover the real heart of the land — and the people.

Once we'd earned our money, and had time to become marginally less confused with the way of life, we took off and immediately found ourselves in the middle of an annual gathering of Samurai Warriors in a small mountainous country town. This was out first experience of a Japanese festival, and we stayed fascinated until the huge array of lanterns hanging in the trees were lit at dusk and the drums started beating for the evening dancing and drinking.

If there's a nation on the planet that cannot hold its liquor, it must be the Japanese above everyone else. It's hilarious to see the sombre-suited city businessmen weaving their blissfully happy way along the underground station subways with a delirious grin on their faces as they clutch onto their colleagues. And you know this is the result of two (maybe three) daring halves of lager.

A fisherman patiently waits while his colleagues walk with nets along the shore of Lake Biwa in Japan.

During our travels, we spent some time in a Zen Buddhist training temple (one of only 40) where we were honoured by an interview with the Grand Master. It was amazing to meet this unostentatious man having seen him working in the garden beforehand, and taken him for a mere gardener. The discipline in his temple was extremely austere with a great deal of fasting, chanting, and praying. However, when we enquired if this was *the* way to attain the heights for which they were striving, we were told that there was no 'only' way, and if we chose, we could find an equally good path to Nirvana via baseball, music, or any other suitable pursuit.

Our adventures in Japan would fill a book, not part of a chapter. However, one further experience ought to be included before we move on to Malaysia and India.

On the Southern Island of Kyushu, we saw the end of the incredibly lovely cherry-blossom season which had been moving slowly south at about the same pace as we were moving. We had passed through the ancient capital of Kyoto and spent days wandering through the myriad of shrines, temples, formal gardens, and lakes.

Our route had followed the coastline, and we'd seen the famous Miki-moto cultured pearl farms, wandered through the streets of tiny fishing villages, and watched the local farmers planting endless rows of rice-plants in the waterlogged paddy-fields. Having decided to take an inland scenic highway to the active volcano appropriately called Mount Aso, and as it was continuously drizzling on that day, we stopped off to camp on a small beach for the rest of the day. There was no point in taking a specially scenic route when you could barely see the road in front of you as it disappeared into the low grey cloud and foggy rain.

We stayed in the van and wrote lengthy letters. As dusk came, we cooked our evening meal, and then retired to an early bed.

At about two o'clock the next morning, we both shot bolt upright in terror. Someone was trying to overturn our van — and presumably flush us out.

Having been on the road for 2½ years by now, and not having had any kind of attack, this, we reckoned, was it. The van was being rocked ferociously from side to side. Things were falling out of cupboards above us. Our whole world was collapsing, as we clung to each other in fright.

The Pagoda of Toji Temple (Near Kyoto the cultural heart and old capital of Japan). One of the joys of being a self contained overlander in Japan is the wealth of small country shrines, castles and temples that proliferate in the wooded interior — away from the industrial coastlines.

Simultaneously, a thought struck both of us: to rock the van to this extent, we'd surely hear a load of grunting and panting with the strain. But there was utter silence. A terrible silence.

The rocking continued as fiercely as ever, and I suddenly remembered our South American experience. We were in the middle of not just a tremor, but a massive 'quake. And that was even more scary than a gang of Japanese thieves rocking our van.

Suddenly the rocking stopped, and we could hear the peaceful lapping of the waves on the seashore a few feet away. Everything was calm, and a gentle silence took over from the awful silence of before.

The next morning we set off on a clear-skied, sunny day to take the scenic route to Mount Aso. We got as far as the first tollgate. It was lying across the road, a shattered mountain of concrete and girders.

Further on, we were told, the highway had been completely swept away by a gigantic landslide caused by the earthquake which had been a big one (force 6.4 on the Richter scale) and which had been less than ten kilometres from where we were parked. However, we consoled ourselves that, had we set off the day before, we might have been parked exactly on the spot that was now several hundred meters below where it *should* be.

And so, finally, the day of our departure dawned. We were leaving the country so steeped in culture and history that it is impossible to encapsulate it in a few mere paragraphs. It is a country that for one brief period in its history closed its doors to ALL foreigners for longer than the United States has existed in total. We were saying goodbye to a nation which in many ways was remarkably similar to our own island nation. We were on our way again, in a tiny Japanese freighter that hadn't had a passenger (let alone a foreigner) treading its scruffy decks for over ten years.

The cupboard we were allocated housed some friendly cockroaches, as did the electric toaster that sat on our breakfast table beneath the sticky fly trap that was covered with tiny corpses. Even so, toast and greasy egg was the only concession we were given, as something had told the ship's cook that even *we* couldn't stomach a breakfast of seaweed like the rest of the crew.

The remainder of the meals were the same as the crew's and we thanked our maker that we had a plentiful supply of apples and biscuits for the ten-day voyage through the typhoon-ridden (but miraculously calm) seas to Singapore.

The period we spent on the Malay peninsula was a bad one for us. We had been travelling too long, and were somewhat weary. The weather was frequently wet, and always depressingly humid. Nevertheless, we enjoyed the spell in Thailand more than any of the other parts of this long strip of land.

Because we couldn't drive through Burma to India, we had to back-track to Penang to catch the huge ferry to India. We were on a piece of land that was physically connected to Calais, which was only a short ferry-ride from England, and we had had enough of travelling.

Originally we had set out with a maximum of three years as our travelling time, and this period was almost up. We wanted to get home, and felt somewhat depressed that we were still so far away from friends and family.

However, India put an end to this brief spell of depression.

Like almost every overland traveller, we passionately loved India while at the same time passionately loathing her.

We arrived in Madras on November the second. It was a public holiday. We'd eaten curry for breakfasts, lunches and suppers on the grossly overcrowded ship along with the passengers and crew. Our fingers were stained bright yellow — cutlery was unheard of — and we longed to get off the docks and stock up with local foodstuffs to cook for ourselves.

However, this was not to be. The great God Curry had destined us to remain with the van, shut in the docks until the holiday was over. And the only food we had was a can of tuna, some rice, and an ample supply of curry powder... We had curry, and went to bed.

India hit us like a great hot stinking polluted oven. The chaos and confusion on the streets was unimaginable. Bicycles, animals, carts, ancient cars and buses roared and rumbled in all directions with no apparent control. Thankfully it was slow, but nevertheless it was a degree of confusion we had never encountered before.

Gradually we learned the necessary techniques, which apply throughout the whole of India, and which cannot be taught by proxy. The *only* way to learn is to do it — but do it with caution at all times, blowing your horn continuously as you do.

The loveliness of India is predominantly in the South. Here, there is more ancient history, culture, dancing, music and flowers than the most ardent culture-vulture could desire. The problem is moving to and from each burst of beauty or history. The roads are generally poor-to-appalling, and are used as meeting places for dogs, monkeys, camels, cows, bullocks, and chatting bunches of humans. Crowds abound everywhere, and in the three months we were there, we never ever were able to stop and have a quick snack-lunch in the wildest seemingly-uninhabited bit of countryside without having the van surrounded by the time we'd taken our first bite.

Modern India is a veritable nightmare. It is a constant surprise that anything works. If you buy a box of matches, you can be sure of two results: Not one will ignite OR the first one you strike will cause the entire box to explode in your hand. If you buy a bottle of fruit squash, it's pretty certain you'll have to smash the neck to get at the contents as the top appears to have been welded on. The process of buying (say) a mere cabbage in a superstore is a happening that requires the patience of Job. Here's how it's done:

1) Go to one of the stalls and join the queue.
2) When your turn finally comes, choose a cabbage.
3) Wait while a bill is laboriously written out.
4) Offer your money, have it refused, get told to pay 'over there'.
5) Leave the cabbage, take the bill, and join the queue 'over there'.
6) When your turn finally comes, pay, get a laboriously-written-out receipt, and return to the original stall.
7) Get sent (politely) to the end of the queue.
8) When your turn finally comes, hand over the receipt for your money.
9) Wait while it is rubber stamped (again) and collect your cabbage which, like you, is visibly wilting by now.

If you now want to buy a can of condensed milk, you start the whole procedure over again.

The two faces of India: **Above** - when you stop (anywhere in India) the windows of the van are rapidly eclipsed by peering faces. This is a typical though small crowd on the outskirts of Bombay. **Below** - The peace and tranquility of one of the more remote Southern temples (near Mysore) where all the magic and mysticism of ancient India blossoms (despite the turmoil of modern India) to reveal the poetry and grandeur that makes the sub-continent unique.

This is what the British left behind when they finally got out of India. They left everything that is horrendously awful about the Civil Service. They left rubber stamps. They left queues. They left hierarchy. They left unbreakable rules and regulations, the purposes of which have long been forgotten but which will remain enforced until India finally and irrevocably sinks beneath the waves under an all-encompassing mountain of un-attended-to paperwork.

It sound petty and trivial to moan about such things in a land that has fascinated the world for so many centuries. The trouble is, it is not the occasional isolated event or three, it is an unending tidal wave of idiocy that slowly and surely wears you down until you are reduced to a half-crazed jibbering idiot that will do anything to get out of the place. The magic is swamped. The incredible beauty of the Hindu temples is marred. The pressures of the interminable stares from idle adolescents as they eclipse every inch of light from every window in the vehicle every time you stop is eventually intolerable. It is the crowd that goes shopping with you and watches, fascinated, as you buy six eggs from a roadside stall that finally breaks you. And it is the endless string of questions: where do you come from? What is the purpose of your visit? Where are you going? What is your work? that is the last straw.

One Dutch couple painted the answer to these and at least twelve other standard questions on the side of their van to vent their frustration — to no avail, of course.

The one place that is unique in that you are left alone is the small ex-Portuguese state of Goa. Here, everything that is magic about India comes to life. There are miles of golden beaches. Small boys call, selling honey, bread, milk, and paw-paws. The coconut palms drip coconuts. The sea is full of king-sized prawns which cost a pittance from the nearby fishing village. And virtually every foreigner can stroll naked amongst the clothed fishermen without causing a head to turn.

We pulled into this haven and fell in love with it. We knew that we must stay several days here, even though we were aiming to get to the Taj Mahal for the next full moon.

It was over five full weeks before we could bear to move on — for the *following* full moon. Our third Christmas day had been spent in the shade of the palms, sharing a dish from each of the small number of overland vehicles who had gathered there.

Chinese style fishing nets at Cochin (S. India). When the rivers are in flood the nets are hauled up and left unused until the vast quantities of greenery floating downstream have disappeared and the nets lift up fish rather than weeds.

75

There were various 'hippies' in the area, but they left the over-landers alone — as we left them alone. We did little other than eat, snooze, swim, and — as the giant ball of orange sank slowly into the sea each evening — sip a glass of the local brew and take bets as to whether the inevitable sailing dhow would cross the sun as it sank over the shimmering blue horizon.

As seasoned travellers by now, we wondered if the Taj would be a bit of a let-down. Generally speaking, we had become extremely discriminating about man-made wonders, though we were still in awe of natural ones.

We got to Agra just in time and waited the rest of the evening until dark before entering the grounds of the Taj. It was staggering. No amount of tourists flashing their cameras at the moon-lit loveliness could spoil its elegant serenity. No guides spieling off their patter to busloads of tourists could destroy the exquisite magic. It was quite lovely.

Back the following day, it appeared shabby and a trifle squalid after our first sight by full moon, in the same way that the spectacle of Las Vegas by night had become dreadfully scruffy by day.

Despite the fact that after a couple of months of battling with India was beginning to take its toll, we had to include Bombay, and Varanasi (Benares) on the holy river Ganges.

To punctuate the pressures, we took a brief spell in the mountains of Nepal, and returned refreshed to the humid plains of India.

Like good tourists, we gaped at the burning bodies on the banks of the Ganges. We boggled at the human misery in the 'cages' of Bombay where women were to be had for as little as a few cents. And suddenly, we had to go. We had to get out and away from the pressures as rapidly as possible. Three months was all we could take. And we went.

Now, in retrospect, it's a place that calls us back with the same power that the Sahara does. There is something about both these vast areas that gets under your skin and calls and calls and calls. Maybe one day we will return... We'd like to.

And so, the last long leg of our trip began. Muslim Countries merged into each other as we sped Westwards. A month in Pakistan. The unique fascination of Afghanistan... Iran... Turkey... and back into Europe.

On the 5th of June 1976 we crossed Westminster Bridge in the gentle evening sunlight, and we were home. Our van had taken us right around the planet, and we were changed people. Perhaps wiser, and certainly more experienced. We wanted to share our experiences, but few people cared. There'd been a great programme on the box last night, and Mrs Jones' next door neighbour was causing a lot of trouble these days, and my goodness... the price of bread since you both went away on your holiday... Did you have a nice time, then? It's so good to have you home.

And then: oblivion.

We ran. Ran down to Dorset, where we could hide away. Screen ourselves from the "do come to dinner and tell us ALL about it... yes *we* had a wonderful holiday in Spain last year... did we tell you about it... well, hasn't the evening flown, and we've hardly heard a *thing* about your travels... well, never mind... there's always next time you come round..."

We were home. And now, a new life was beginning. And *others* were making plans to take off. Maybe they would make all the mistakes we had. Or some new ones? A little book of objective advice might be of some use?

And so it was born.

5. Planning

The essence of overland travel is the freedom to move both where and when one wishes. Planning the forthcoming trip is therefore advisable only if a considerable amount of flexibility is built in. Nevertheless, that does not mean that one can avoid the inevitable grind of organisation and research so as to avoid being inadequately equipped for what lies ahead.

5.1. Maps

In most areas en route you can pick up adequate road maps from one of four sources: a) at border posts. b) from tourist offices. c) in bookstores or news stands in towns. d) from travellers coming in the opposite direction. Although these are not always reliable sources, you do not need to kit yourself out with all maps for your entire journey. Play it by ear, and bear in mind that the richer the country the greater the choice of maps. The USA is truly amazing.

For Africa, all the maps you will probably need are the set of excellent Michelin ones: Nos 153, 154 and 155. In addition, you may find Nos 169 and 990 useful.

Asia is well covered. One of the best is 'Asia Overland' published by Roger Lascelles. For the direct route from Europe to Singapore, the United Nations Asian Highway series of three strip maps are packed with information, though the centre section through North India and Burma is not available as the Burmese have still not opened up for overland travel. These maps are officially free. In India you can also get somewhat out-of-date strip maps for your particular route from the nearest AA office.

Petrol stations (especially Esso) are sometimes a good source of cheap maps, though they were frequently out of stock in South America. This was compensated by some fairly good tourist offices.

The biggest disadvantage of picking up maps en route is that you occasionally have to travel some distance into the country before finding a good one. However, trying to equip yourself before you start will be both difficult and expensive. Nevertheless, garner what you can from the AA or RAC.

5.2. Books

There are numerous guide books of all kinds on the market. You can spend a small fortune if you start panicking and buying these ad lib. A comprehensive local library *may* give you some ideas, but a visit to some of the trek-type travel clubs will probably be your best bet if you can avoid being roped in to join all of them.

Of all publications for overlanders, one of the best (in our opinion) was the South American Handbook, known to travellers in that part of the world as 'The Bible'. It is published annually by Trade & Travel Publications Ltd., but there is no counterpart for Asia or Africa.

There is also a section at the back of this book which should be perused for additional information to aid the would-be overlander to unearth the information he/she requires.

HMSO produces free booklets on virtually every country in the world in a series entitled 'Hints to businessmen'. They are well worth looking at if you ask them to send you the copies by post. The travel group 'Trail Finders' produce some comprehensive, though fairly expensive, information, and there are probably dozens more sources if you start off with these leads. (*See section 15 for address.*)

Apart from their story-value, books in the 'I rode round the world on a camel' or 'Supertrek adventures to the foothills of the Himalayas' category are not much help. The authors usually indulge themselves in a giant ego-trip, and may scare the pants off you with all the 'desperately dangerous' things that happened to them.

It is essential to take a manual on your vehicle with you. The illustrated and fairly thorough ones are the best. Even if you don't understand yours, someone who does will be able to use it and help you sort out your particular problem. For VWs, Clymer Publications do one of the better ones. There is also the 'Idiots guide to VWs' and 'How to keep your VW alive' which are amusing as well.

The Ross Institute publication 'Preservation of personal health in warm climates' is old-fashioned but quite good. However, the best-buy is 'The Travellers' Health Guide' (published by Roger Lascelles).

5.3. Research

Extensive research into your journey is not essential. Too much information can eliminate the surprise element that is part of the fun of travelling. However, too little is just as bad, and you can miss out on much that is worthwhile en route. With time, cunning, ingenuity and patience (some of the ingredients you will need plenty of once on the road) you can uncover all the information you require — outside the covers of this book.

When you write letters requesting information, be very brief and list your questions numerically. Organisations such as your vehicle manufacturer, tyre or petrol companies, embassies, the Red Cross, WHO, travel clubs, and the AA or RAC are usually inundated with mail, so a clear, concise and brief letter will really help, as will a stamped addressed (large) envelope and/or an International Reply Coupon.

If you wish to write to us, please enclose a large stamped addressed envelope (or International Reply Coupons) if you want a reply. Sorry, but we are not millionaires!

5.4. Languages

School French or better is very useful in many parts of Africa where the alternative in ex-French colonies is either Arabic or a local African tongue.

In South America it is definitely advisable to speak some Spanish. Even 'Spanglish' won't get you far. Very few folk speak more than a couple of words of English and, unlike Portuguese, Spanish is quite an easy language to learn. Without a smattering of it you will miss much, so the effort is worthwhile. W.H. Allen's *'Spanish Made Simple'* is one of the better books to give you a start.

It is unlikely that you will need any language (other than French and Spanish) to get you by. In Japan, unless you are going to spend a long time there, the prospect of learning even a few hundred of the basic *'kanji'* just to be able to read a newspaper is somewhat daunting. However, the Japanese are extremely friendly and often wish to practise the English they·learned at school, so there is a good chance that someone will come to your aid if you stand looking lost with a map in your hand for a few moments.

On the trans-Asia route, it is advisable to learn the basic Farsi numerals before you arrive in Iran. Few people speak English and, unlike the Japanese, they are not averse to fleecing you. Often. Phonetically, the numbers are: 1:*Yek,* 2:*Do,* 3:*Se,* 4:*Chahar,* 5:*Panj,* 6:*Shish,* 7:*Haft,* 8:*Hasht,* 9:*Noh,* 10:*Dah.* Visually, although the numbers can vary somewhat, it is quite important that you learn to recognise them quickly if you don't want to feel like you've just landed from Mars. See also the two photographs on page 113.

As a last resort other than shouting extra loud(!) you can usually get by with sign language and a bit of acting. However, we don't wish on you the experience we once had, trying to describe an egg by acting it out to a bunch of incredulous locals in a small shop in the Iranian countryside. Wow!

A veritable garden of Eden. One of the palm trees just below the spot selected for a brief stopover — which turned out to last five beautiful weeks, in Goa (on the West coast of India).
Nearly all the visiting overlanders wore no clothes, and Jonathan, a true conformist at heart, didn't want to set a precedent by reversing the trend ...

6. The Vehicle

6.1. Type

There is a wide range of vehicles to choose from: VWs, Land Rovers, Ford Transits, Citroens, Mercedes, Bedfords and so on. We know of one German guy who spent sixteen or more years continuously on the road on a bicycle! In Colombia, we met a man from Argentina who, with two dogs and a donkey, was walking from Buenos Aires to New York ... He'd been going for two years, and reckoned he was about half way. We also met an Austin seven (1937) that had been virtually everywhere in the world.

By far the most popular vehicle is the VW bus, but your personal choice will be dictated by your requirements, your budget, and your destination. A left-hand-drive vehicle will have to be converted to RHD if it is to remain in Australia permanently. Diesel engines are becoming increasingly popular, especially on the Asia run, because of the simplified mechanics of the engine and the often horrific price of fuel. Diesel is usually a lot cheaper than gasoline. High power/performance should be of little or no interest to you, but bear in mind that a diesel van may prove to be less economical than *two* carefully converted, compact vehicles (2CV or Renault 4) travelling together.

In our opinion, towing any sort of trailer is a very bad idea for overland travel. Apart from being cumbersome, and difficult to manoeuvre, you may need an additional *'carnet'* for it, thus preventing you from dumping *en route* once you have realised what a nightmare it is, or once it has started to fall apart on the rough roads. Also, do not be tempted to do the trip 'in style' in a big vehicle. These may be fine for Europe, Australia, or North America, but elsewhere they will be a real headache and frequently an embarrassment to you. (In most poor countries you will be painfully aware of the huge gulf between the possessions of the local people and your own 'mobile palace' — even in a VW.)

As can be seen by the map on page 160 of our route in a standard VW bus, four-wheel-drive is not necessary unless you intend to explore particularly remote off-the-beaten-track terrain. Do *not* be advised to the contrary.

When you are choosing a vehicle, bear in mind two important factors: Space and spaciousness. The bigger the vehicle, the more space you have, and you will inevitably fill every nook and cranny. Result: fuel consumption will go up due to excess weight, more roads will be impassable to you; extraction from soft sand or mud will be more of a problem; getting a tow out will be less easy; and shipping the brute will be incredibly expensive.

On the other hand *spaciousness* is important. Living in a 2CV or Renault 4, or even a Land Rover, can be very cramped. Particularly in bad weather. The design of your interior living area is critical and, if you can achieve a real feeling of spaciousness by being inventive, you will have the perfect vehicle — whatever make it is.

Bear in mind that availability of spares and service is most important. Unless you are mechanically minded, the less international the make of vehicle, the more problems you will encounter. Even with its proud (and usually, but not always justified) boast of 'world-wide' service facilities, the VW is virtually unrepresented in Argentina or India. In Mexico and Brazil, the (locally made) Volkswagens are very different in both engine and body, so spares for European models can be a big headache. As a general rule, the less sophisticated and more basic your engine, the better off you are. Thus, the VW 1800 cc engine is not as advisable as the more simple and well known 1600 cc version.

Air-cooled motors are highly susceptible to dust, but water-cooled ones can boil, freeze and leak. Nobody's perfect! The rear-mounted VW engine can easily be damaged by boulders etc. but protection plates can be made (from VW-supplied templates) if you wish. Most of your success, however, will be derived from sensible, moderate, and careful driving, rather than a heap of mechanical devices such as four-wheel-drive, locking differentials and so on.

A winch is not necessary. But it is advisable to have a good strong towing point on both front and back of the vehicle. Take a sturdy cable with you. Where there are roads, or even tracks, help (of sorts) will come along sooner or later. Be prepared to accept *and to give* it.

If your vehicle is in good mechanical condition, even if it's very old, and is spacious to live in, you cannot go very far wrong.

6.2. The conversion
Converting a vehicle to be a home-on-wheels is always very personal. Time and distance will determine your requirements. Pre-fabricated conversions are designed for short holidays and weekends, and are usually for four or more people. Much home-made adaptation will be necessary for a long trip just for two people.

To start from scratch with an empty van and do it yourself may be cheaper, but it will take a lot of time and effort. If you intend to increase your fuel-carrying capacity, consider building in an extra fuel tank as an alternative to jerry cans, but make sure it is sound if you get it from a breaker's yard. You will need extra fuel capacity in Africa, but no other main routes in the world other than for fuel economies when entering countries where fuel is expensive.

If you have a permanently high roof, you will have more wind resistance and higher shipping costs, but you will have more storage space (do you really need it?) and the possibility of a gravity-fed water supply which can be nice. Whatever you do, you will be continually surprised by the inventiveness of the other travellers you meet on the road.

The following 18 sub-sections should help you in preparing a comfortable conversion for either a long or short journey:

6.2.1. Lift-up (pop-top) roof:
Unless you are a midget, or wish to become a hunchback, the value of being able to stand up inside the van cannot be over-estimated. Various types and sizes are available, and a good place to see them all is at one of the Camping or Motoring Exhibitions in London. These roofs, however, can be expensive and, if your budget is a bit tight, consider cutting a hole in the roof, and superimposing the top half of the body of a small saloon car from a local breaker's yard. Although weird to look at, it is aerodynamic, and the windows give visibility and light while being fairly thief-proof.

6.2.2. Bed:
A bed that doubles as a daytime seat is the best arrangement. Conversion should be as easy as possible. Avoid screw-on legs unless the screw threads are really sturdy. Plan the position in the van so that you leave some standing room for undressing when the bed is made up, as mosquitoes, rain, and crowds of staring locals often prevent undressing outside, and the front cab may be stacked with a pile of your 'daytime' stuff. The expense of good quality, down-filled sleeping bags is worthwhile, and bag-type sheet/liners will ease cleaning problems.

Loose cushions can double as pillows and sheepskin car seat-covers are invaluable as extra bed-covers in cold weather while eliminating the horror of trying to sit on plastic front seats that have been in the fierce sun. Many trans-Africa Land Rover travellers increase their living space by making a fold-up tent unit on hinged hoops with a removable centre strut, mounted on a large roof-rack. Provided it's watertight by day, and mosquito-proof by night, it permits travel with a permanently made-up bed. Two spare tyres can be fitted between the roof and the roof-rack and the centre of gravity is kept very low.

6.2.3. Table:
A free-standing fold-away table or, better still, a clip-on table with a drop-down leg, is essential. The latter clipped to a side wall of the van, gives the most space inside and can be made free-standing, for outside use, if you bring four screw-on legs with you. A good storage place for the table is on runners hanging below some roof cupboards. One or two compact folding aluminium chairs are useful for eating outside, and for long stopovers in good weather.

6.2.4. Storage:
The more space you have, the more gear you'll take. Basic requirements are:

a) Clothes storage. An absolute minimum is needed for travelling (*see 13.8.*)

b) Foodstuffs. A general store cupboard or chest, plus a place for the daily items such as salt/pepper pots, tea, coffee, sugar, spices, cutlery, crockery etc. N.B. Rattles can drive you mad.

c) Night things. Sleeping bags, sheets, pillowcases etc.

d) General purpose. Books, cameras, medicines, tools, cassettes and so on.

When building cupboards make them strong, but of light materials. They should be lockable, even if you aren't going to ship the vehicle. Similarly because of thieves, if you've a roof-rack it must be sturdy and both water and thief-proof. Avoid storing very heavy things high up, to prevent the vehicle becoming top-heavy.

6.2.5. Windows:

Many travellers like to have plenty of windows for maximum light and visibility. However these must be able to be completely blocked out with curtains or sliding wood or metal panels, both for privacy and security. Others prefer virtually no windows in the living area, giving more storage space and privacy (especially good in India) but a very dark interior.

Apart from an unforseeable bit of plain bad luck, you should not run into many rock-throwing small boys other than in the Eastern part of Turkey where, covering the outside of your windows with corrugated card and/or plastic bags for two or three days is well worth the trouble. If you get caught in a fierce sandstorm, a thick coat of wax on all windward glass can prevent it from being sand-blasted.

6.2.6. Air circulation (natural):

Louvre windows (bought or home-made) provide an excellent cross-draught in hot weather. They are the most thief-proof too. Hinged or sliding windows are the easiest entry points for burglars by day or night. Beware. Mosquito screens will be necessary in most parts of the world. (Tip: Sew Velcro-strip on the border of each net, and glue the counterpart strip around each door or window for easy putting up and taking down.) A roof-vent is a very good idea but, even with this air circulation, you should insulate the roof interior to protect against heat and, more important, to reduce condensation which, in humid weather, can be awful.

6.2.7. Air circulation (artificial):

An electric fan, or two if the budget allows, is a marvellous comfort during sweltering hot nights. By day when moving, normal air circulation of air through open windows is enough. An air-conditioner is a luxury which, if you can afford it, may give you some hours of comfort. The time you need cooling, however, is when you are stopped and the engine is not running ...

6.2.8. Gas Storage:

Butane/Propane gas is the most common method for cooking, heating, or running a fridge. A fridge, using gas 24 hours, will consume approximately three kilos of gas in a fortnight. A small cooker will use about the same in warm weather, and more in cold. Heaters use the most, even if used sparingly. As you are travelling in a mobile bomb at the best of times, it is neither advisable nor necessary to carry huge quantities of gas with you. It is very common, and you should not need to hump more than a total of 4-5 week's-worth at any time. However, as the European-style 'exchange-bottle' system is rare outside Europe, it is essential that you take an adaptor for filling bottles (*see 11.3*).

There is no truly safe place to store your gas bottles. A leak if they're inside the van can be dangerous, but placed at the front or the back on the outside could be even worse in the event of an accident. Mounting them on the roof is also problematical as they can make you top-heavy, and the necessarily long pipes can chafe and wear on bumpy roads. Wherever you put them, make sure all connections are sound and from time to time are checked. Take some gas-pipe thread-sealing tape with you as well. And remember, as liquid gas is heavier than air, it will sink to the bottom of the  storage box in the event of a leak — so make sure that there is an escape hole which can be sealed with a rubber bung to prevent dust coming in when on the move. This should be removed for a few hours every few days in case of a leak and a build up of gas. Some sort of adaptor to convert the **small** filling hole of a Gaz bottle to a larger size used by the large depots is most advisable. (See 'Gas supplies)

6.2.9. Cooker:

A variety of cookers is available at all good camping shops. One with two burners and a grill is ideal. An oven, even if used for storage when not in use, is space consuming and hardly necessary. (in remote areas such as deep in the jungle, where bread is rare, you can 'improvise' an oven: one small pan or tin to contain the dough, standing on three pebbles in about 1cm of oil, inside a larger pan with a lid, and placed on a burner for about half an hour, makes fairly good bread — or cake.) Non-stick camping pans are great, and a pressure cooker is highly economical. If you run out of gas or want to go trekking, a small portable petrol-stove is a useful accessory, if your vehicle is petrol-powered.

6.2.10. Heater:

A small gas heater, provided it is safe, can be good in cold weather evenings, and essential in freezing temperatures. Countries like Turkey and Canada can easily go as low as -40°C in winter at night. Even in such extremes, it is highly dangerous to sleep with the heater on, even with good ventilation.

There is a petrol-driven heater unit accessory for VWs (mounted in the engine compartment) but these are very expensive, and can rapidly drain the battery as the van's generator is not charging when the main engine is not running. The American 'white gas' heaters are not much use outside the US as the highly refined fuel is difficult to find elsewhere.

6.2.11. Water storage:

A high roof allows a water bottle to be mounted to give a gravity-fed water supply. This is pleasant, but a manual or foot operated pump is quite adequate. Electric pumps are convenient but can, and often do, go wrong ... Several small (ten litre) bottles are more easy to fill than one or two big ones, if the tap is in an awkward place. For two people, a thirty or forty litre capacity should be enough for normal travelling, though in Africa you should have more. Even if you build in a large capacity, it is crazy to drag big quantities of water with you as you travel. On the entire journey, we *never* carried more than 70 litres, although we had a purifier which gave us the possibility of re-cycling our water in the event of a breakdown or delay in places like the Sahara.

Collapsible plastic water bottles are available. They do not stand up to constant use as well as rigid ones, but are a good idea as a reserve capacity when the nearest water is far away and you want to fill up for a long stopover on some lonely beach, or to do the washing. (*See also 13.1*)

6.2.12. Sink:

Although you can get by with a bowl, a built-in sink with a drain outlet under the vehicle is well worth while. Available space will dictate its size and position. The drain outlet should be as curve-free as possible, and the hole underneath sealed around the pipe to stop excess dust coming into the interior. A supplementary washing up bowl is useful, particularly if the sink is very small. You will often use it for clothes washing, or body-washing when you cannot find a shower.

6.2.13. Shower:

You can usually seek out a shower at main line railway terminals, medium-quality hotels, campsites, public baths and so on. The route through Asia is not much of a problem, but Africa and South America are a little more difficult as there are very few campsites. A good body-wash in your plastic bowl will usually tide you over. Forget about trying to build a shower into a small van. With a bit of imagination/improvisation, it is possible to make up a sort of shower thus: ingredients: 1 foot-pump, 1 bucket or water-container such as a bowl, 1 length (3 metres) of thin-bore flexible tubing, 1 'Y' joint to fit into the tubing. Connect one end of the tubing to the footpump, and make the other end into a circular (collar) loop that will hang around your neck. Pierce the loop with small holes so that when the water is pumped up the pipe, it escapes around your neck and runs down your body. If you ain't got a foot-pump, the system works as well by gravity if the water source is above your head.

6.2.14. Toilet:

Most of the time you will be travelling in open country, and toilet facilities will not normally be a problem. Some sort of toilet can usually be located in time in built-up areas. If you think French public loos are bad, wait until you've travelled overland for a while. You get quickly hardened to the most unbelievably primitive and filthy systems, and often prefer the nearby bushes. In the event of a bad dose of the 'Teheran trots' or the 'Inca quickstep', you can always improvise something temporarily with drawn curtains and a plastic bag. In our opinion, the most compact fold-away loo is not worth the space it takes, and we jettisoned ours very early on. Toilet paper can be scarce, so always keep a running stock of a few spare rolls.

6.2.15 Fridge:

In hot or tropical climates, a small fridge in the van can be wonderful. Apart from preserving some fresh foods and keeping a can of margarine from turning to oil, the pleasure of drinking cool water in the intense midday heat is indescribable. Although not essential, a fridge is one of the last things we would have sacrificed. There are many models to choose from if you can track them down.

Usually they operate on a three-way system of camping gas, 12v or mains electricity, using the heat-exchange system. They have to be reasonably level to work efficiently. The alternative compressor-types are more expensive to buy, and can quickly drain the battery if you are stopped for several days without moving. Top-opening fridges have a lot less cold-loss when opened and are usually more compact. You do not need a big fridge.

If you operate yours on gas, make sure that it has an automatic cut-out in case the flame should blow out and, if your van is reasonably airtight, you should have a proper outlet for the chimney. As some gas can be very poor quality, you will probably need a small bottle-brush to clean the soot from the chimney now and then. Water evaporation 'coolers' are a poor though cheaper alternative, and rarely work well, if at all, in the fierce heat you will encounter.

6.2.16 Lighting
As in a house, good interior lighting can make living in the van a lot more pleasant. The fluorescent type of tube lights are most economical, and give a bright but very harsh light. Supplementary tungsten lights, such as flexible-stalk map-reading lights create a much nicer atmosphere. A very small clip-on inspection light is also useful in the living area. (*See also 6.5.*)

6.2.17 Audio:
Because of their small size, cassette tapes are most popular. If music is at all important to you, it is great to have a built-in player with a good sound; four speakers if possible. Try mounting two in the front door panels, and two at the rear. A headphone jack socket is also worth installing so that one person can 'rock on' while the other has silence. A portable tape recorder can help create as vivid memories of the journey as photographs do, and a tape of messages to or from home can be fun.

A combination of AM (medium wave) and SW (short wave) radio is by far the best. FM radio stations are still pretty rare, and long wave (LW) is virtually useless. The BBC World Service on SW and occasionally MW can be picked up with a bit of patience in most places, and many British Embassies provide the free programme guide and details called 'London calling'. Make sure that your external antenna is as inaccessible as possible. Small boys, and fully grown ones too, seem to have an irresistible passion for bending or breaking them. Forget TV. It's nice to escape anyway, and a British set won't work on those funny foreign systems.

6.2.18. Tent:
Don't take one unless you plan to go trekking frequently, or unless there are more than two of you and you plan to use it nightly. They are bulky to store, and it will probably be more trouble than it's worth. A tent also virtually eliminates the possibility of a quick get-away in the unlikely event of trouble. However, a permanently fixed roll-out canopy over the main door is an excellent idea, as it can extend your living area quickly and easily to provide pleasant shade from the sun as well as from the rain. Make sure it is fixed securely for rough-road driving.

If the legs on the above illustration are staked into the ground, they'll provide additional access into the van for insects. Make sure that the rolled up canopy is secure when motoring at speed.

6.3. Weatherproofing
Rain is perhaps the most unpleasant weather of all to travel in. Leaks from lift-up roofs, drips from condensation, steamed-up windows, and damp clothes or bedding can affect morale more rapidly than intense heat or freezing cold. Prepare for this, and bring some tubes of clear flexible sealant, and a few cans of anti-fog condensation spray. Washing-up liquid wiped on also works well.

6.4. Engine
Take great care of your engine, and forget that AA-type rescue services and competent mechanics exist. It will pay you to learn the basics about your engine and do your own lubrication and general maintenance in most parts of the world. Your chances of ending up with cross-threaded plugs will perhaps be reduced. Practice before you set off, with the aid of a good workshop manual.

With a VW engine, you should particularly watch that a) The valves are kept properly adjusted. It's not difficult once you know how. b) The air cleaner is well maintained. Dust can do a lot of damage to your engine. c) The engine oil is changed at least as often as the manufacturer recommends and 'rubbish' oils at bargain prices in local markets are avoided. Above all, bear in mind that mechanics abroad will be utterly baffled by sophisticated mechanical devices that are taken for granted in the West when/if you need work doing on your engine. Things like fuel injection are still unheard of in many places you will be visiting. (*See also 6.7.*). For air-cooled engines, a piece of netting soaked in oil across the external air intake-vents will allow adequate air to pass through, yet trap a sizeable proportion of dust when travelling on dry dusty roads. Though the net needs to be cleaned *daily*.

6.5. Electrical

Although there are some compact petrol-driven generators on the market, a simpler, cheaper and quieter alternative is to carry two good batteries. Invest in big ones with long (over 100) amp hours if possible. False economy in this area is really silly, as you will depend on your batteries for a very great deal. Wire them into the system in parallel and fit an adequately powerful on/off switch for each one as opposed to the automatic switch-over devices on the market. By doing this you will have: a) worry-free use of plenty of electricity when stopped for long periods, or at night, with a full battery for starting in the morning. b) 'free' electricity as you re-charge while driving. c) The potential of an extra 'kick' for the starter motor in freezing weather by switching both batteries on together, briefly.

Apart from a very small inspection light which is useful as a 'mobile' light in the vehicle, a permanent light mounted in the engine compartment is worth considering. Two or three sockets in strategic positions in the living area are a good idea, with standardised plugs on all electrical gadgets. The most common type are cigarette-lighter sockets.

As a general rule, DO NOT drive at night. It should therefore not be necessary to fit yourself out with spotlights. In any case, they are quite likely to be stolen. Ordinary headlights are more than adequate for the odd time you may have to use them, but if you wish to install quartz halogen lights, they should be protected with metal grilles from flying stones as they will probably be very difficult to replace. Best bet is to be content with normal headlights and nothing else.

6.6. Tyres

In developed areas of the world, tubeless tyres are common. In many other countries they are unknown. If you set off with tubeless tyres, several spare tubes will be needed sooner or later. While radial tyres give considerably better mileage on conventional paved roads, they have a weaker wall than non-radials and can be more easily ripped to ribbons on the often rough, stony, or badly pot-holed roads in Africa or South America. Radials should be o.k. for main roads in Asia. From our, and other travellers' experiences, re-mould tyres are a waste of money as they rarely stand up to the pressures put on them by a heavy vehicle on an overland trip. Eight-ply tyres, though not always available, are worth the extra cost as they are really tough.

One of the best brands on the market are made by a small Swiss company called 'Maloja'. They can be found in Britain, but are not available outside Europe. Truck-type treads hum noisily on paved roads and are quite good in mud but are bad in soft sand as they tend to dig you in rather than out. (Nearly-bald tyres are good in sand.) *Section 11.7.4 covers difficult terrain in more detail.*

Snow chains are useful not only in snow, but also in thick slimy mud, but remember that wherever you go in your vehicle, there will be other vehicles to pull you out if you're stuck. A pair of tyre irons can help in more remote areas where you may have to mend your own punctures. However, in most places you can get them fixed for you, but take plenty of patches if you want the job done properly. One spare tyre is essential. Two is a good idea. If mounted on the outside, *they must be thief-proof.*

6.7. Spares/Accessories

Each traveller has his own idea of what spares to take. You are no exception, and space and priorities will decide for you. However much you take, the bit that goes will probably be the bit you haven't got as a spare. Two German travellers we met in Africa had so many spares, including a complete spare engine, that they had to sleep outside their van. Find a friendly man in a local spares department of a dealer and have a chat with him. Enquire which are the parts that most frequently go, and what he would advise you to take. Lighter, smaller, or more delicate parts are the most advisable (*see 13.2.*).

A compact but well-equipped tool box is a 'must'. Although you may know little about car mechanics, you will probably learn quite a bit during the journey. People have been known to set off for India without even a jack! Take at least one, with an extra metal base plate (about 1ft square) to stop it sinking into soft surfaces.

Of the many accessories you can clutter yourself up with if you yield to the temptations of your local Halfords, there are a few that are strongly advisable: one of these is an *oil temperature gauge.* The thermometer part can be fitted into the dip-stick aperture, with the gauge mounted in a prominent position so that you can keep a continual eye on it while driving. It may save you a major repair bill. An oil warning light is usually a standard fitting on most vehicles, but in the bright sunlight you may not notice it in time to save your bearings. Fitting some sort of buzzer warning instead of or as well as the light is not a difficult task, and is highly advisable. A third gadget that is recommended is a car compass. Signposts are rare both in cities and in the wilds, and it can be a very useful device.

Of the myriad of other accessories that are available, a few worth considering are: a grease gun and a tin of good quality graphite grease, a sturdy foot-pump, a tyre pressure gauge, an extra horn and separate button for the passenger seat (almost essential in India!), a car-voltage soldering iron, touch-up paint in your colours, a magnet, a tube of metal-mender, some gun-gum or firegum, and some masking and insulating tape. Incidentally, we were given an altimeter as a farewell gift and it proved to be one of our most enjoyable 'luxuries'.

6.8. Safety

Mounting a spare tyre on the front of a VW bus does not act as a 'buffer'. Conversely, it localises the point of impact in a head-on crash. To protect your legs somewhat, a local blacksmith can make up an anti-crash bar (a good footrest too) which may possibly help. Laminated windscreens are well worth the money. Even with these, some people make up iron grilles on their windows and travel about looking like a mobile fortress. For the record we did not bother, and although we collected four separate chip marks on the laminated screen, it lasted us the three and a half years perfectly adequately. Maybe we were lucky. The seat-belt habit is a good one.

6.9. Anti-theft

Additional locks on all doors can easily be fitted, and are well worth the expense, particularly if shipping is involved. Quarter-light windows are very easily forced open, and sliding ones are bad in this respect too. Keep all valuable things as hidden from view as possible, as many travellers have been ripped off in broad daylight even while sitting in their vehicle. The chances of having something stolen from you are almost 100%, particularly in Colombia and East Africa.

In hot weather, the temptation to sleep with doors and windows open and only mosquito netting is great. Don't. If you do, you will almost certainly wake up with fewer of your possessions. In the unhappy event of a theft, your money, passports, carnet etc. should be hidden in the most inaccessible place. A good strong cash-box hidden from view inside the vehicle, and bolted or welded from the inside to chassis is a good idea.

Never park and leave the van by day or night unless you are reasonably sure it is in a fairly safe area, and always 'immobilise' it one way or another. Standard burglar alarms are quite good, but your own invented system will possibly be better. A switch that 'kills' all electricity is one way. A steering lock is another. An excellent and very simple scheme is that of *visual deterrents:* Fit hidden brackets that take clip-on bars to go across all windows. They *look* impregnable from the outside, and can easily and quickly be unclipped before you drive away. The bars can be ordinary wood dowel — painted shiny black.

All these precautions may sound paranoiac. They aren't. Theft is one of your greatest problems when on the road, as you clearly have a vehicle stacked with highly saleable goodies. If you take the minimum of things, and are prepared to lose the lot at any time, you will be on the right track.

6.10. Spare keys
It is quite easy to lock yourself out of many vehicles. VWs are no exception. Select a good hiding place and fix a spare key to the exterior of the van. Keep a note of all your key numbers as well.

With a spare wheel mounted at the front we installed an internal foot-rest-cum-anti-crash-bar. Happily we never tested our local blacksmith's engineering - but it kept our feet happy. (See 6.8.)

Double-locks on all doors are advisable: This picture shows our own solution — providing a real and visual deterrent. (See 6.9)

7. Personal

7.1. Medicines and first aid

Take a basic first aid kit with you, plus some disposable needles and alcohol for future cholera injections in the poorer countries where hospital hygiene standards can be extremely low. Your local GP will help you sort out what injections you should have prior to departure, and you'll need proper vaccination certificates for most countries.

Store what (few) medicines you decide to take in the coolest place, and take care that the labels don't rub off with the vibrations of the rough roads. Malaria and water-purifying tablets can be bought at good chemists shops, and 'Lomotil' is extremely effective for dealing with the heavy runs. A great relief for toothache is to mix a small quantity of zinc oxide and oil of cloves into a paste and rub it onto the affected area, so take these ingredients with you. Incidentally, if you wear glasses, it might be worth taking a note of the prescription details with you.

7.2. Drugs

It is possible, and easy, to get very good hash/grass or whatever you want in most countries in the world. You will also possibly find that travelling and all the nice things that go with it make a far better 'trip' than any self-induced one. What you choose to do is your own business anyhow, but *never, ever* attempt to cross a border with any kind of drugs on you or in the vehicle. It really isn't worth the risk, and penalties can include death in some places. If you are giving a lift to a hitch-hiker, insist that he or she goes through the border, with all luggage, entirely independently of you, so *you'll* not be responsible if *they* are breaking local laws.

7.3. Contraception etc.

Take what you need with you. The same applies to things like Tampax which can be either expensive or not available...

7.4. Clothing

Whatever you believe will be necessary will be too much — by about 50%. Border crossings are made easier if you don't look like a hippy, but for the rest of the time you'll need an astonishingly small amount as illustrated in 13.8. You can, and probably will, buy some interesting local clothes as you go. Non-iron things are obviously advisable and, apart from one outfit that can be used for the occasional night out or if you wish to work *en route,* jeans and T-shirts are the ideal travelling gear. (Incidentally, Levis can be useful bartering currency, and can often be sold.) Lastly, in many Moslem countries exposed female flesh can cause provocation to the randy male population, so be sensitive to these customs. One long skirt is advisable, particularly in Africa and Asia.

7.5. Leisure

Even if you don't read much normally, you probably will on the road, especially in the evenings when reading can be one of the more pleasurable pastimes. As with casettes, paperback books are often swapped with other travellers. Also (if you enjoy them) cards, chess and even 'Travel Scrabble' are worth the space they take.

7.6. Photography

Film in foreign countries is usually expensive. Exceptions are places like Hong Kong, Penang, Singapore, the US and Japan. If you buy a lot of films before you leave, investigate obtaining tax-exemption from HM Customs or at least make sure you get a good bulk-buy discount. Films should be stored in a cool place in the van, and processed as soon as possible after exposure. Some of our films had to wait six months as we didn't trust the post in the areas we were in.

Local colour processing can be awful, so it is worth making arrangements before you leave for both processing and dust-free storing at home until you return. A friend who takes on this job will be a good friend indeed. Local processing of black and white film is nearly always o.k. A colour Polaroid camera can smooth your passage through borders by flattering the vanity of the officials, but it is a very expensive form of photography.

Many travellers believe that camera equipment prevents you from really seeing what you are looking at. There is a lot of truth in that, but if you don't take anything with you, you will probably regret it. For the record, we abandoned the idea of movies, and concentrated on colour slides and black and white stills only. We took two 35 mm cameras. Both were bought second hand. They were an Asahi Pentax Spotmatic (1:1.4 50 mm lens) and a Prinzflex Super TTL (1:1.7 55 mm lens). Of the accessories we took with us we would place them in the following order of usefulness: a) 200 mm telephoto lens. b) Tripod and release cable. c) Right-angle lens. d) Times-2 converter. e) Flash equipment.

Although the quality of the shot can suffer a bit, a times-2 converter gave us the permutations of 50 mm, 100 mm, 200 mm and 400 mm lenses. The right-angle lens was great in areas where people were camera-shy. Believing the camera was pointing away from them, they would often become superbly relaxed 'models'. We rarely used the flash equipment, and only missed having a wide-angle lens on a couple of occasions. N.B. Mercury cell light meter batteries can sometimes be extremely difficult to find, so always keep a spare one.

Some readers have found difficulty in tracking this device down. Photocopy this page and send it with your enquiry to a dealer selling a wide range of Japanese cameras and/or the larger manufacturers such as Pentax Cameras.

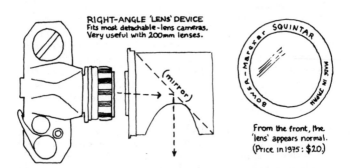

RIGHT-ANGLE 'LENS' DEVICE
Fits most detachable-lens cameras.
Very useful with 200mm lenses.

(mirror)

SQUINTAR
Bowsa—Marexar
MADE IN JAPAN

From the front, the
'lens' appears normal.
(Price in 1975: $20.)

8. Protection

8.1. Weapons

"Take a gun!" they all cried before we left and after their pleas of "don't go" had failed. Many friends sincerely believed that we were crazy to set off around the world without being armed to the teeth.

We didn't take one, and our *strongest possible* advice is 'don't'. If you get into any sort of trouble (and it is not likely unless you are very unlucky or silly) the chances are that you will 'escalate' the situation if you start waving a gun about. Unless you are a crack shot, you will probably be the loser and, if you kill or injure a local inhabitant, you, the foreigner, will be in serious trouble no matter what the circumstances. What's more important, you cannot expect Western concepts of justice to apply. (True story: two travellers who *believed* they were being attacked by some rowdy locals, decided to get rid of them by firing a gun in the air. The locals dispersed — very rapidly. But they returned later that night and shot one of the travellers dead and wounded the other.)

Should a tricky situation arise, keep cool, don't panic, and remember that you are almost certainly more intelligent than the aggressors and can surely outwit them. Some people travel with a 'toy' gun or starting pistol. Although you don't have any problems at borders, we believe this is the worst of both worlds as it can escalate a potentially volatile situation, and yet, if your bluff is called, you are utterly defenceless.

According to how potentially violent a person you are (!) it will be up to you to decide what, if any, weapons to take. Only bring what you are *prepared to use,* whether it is your wits, smoke bombs, firecrackers, aerosol sprays, truncheons, or a roof-mounted intercontinental ballistic missile.

Don't be scared by all this. We never encountered any sort of violence except at the end of our journey in Istanbul, Europe, when a public loo attendant became enraged by an attempt to pee without paying. He attacked with a broom-handle...

8.2. Precautions

8.2.1. Fire: take at least two fire extinguishers with you, and fix them in strategic and highly accessible positions. Periodically check them if possible. They need not be large and cumbersome, but quick reactions on your part will be most essential.

8.2.2. Accidents

Statistically, and from personal experience, Brazil is unsurpassed for suicidal drivers. The Teheran mob must surely be the most stupid. The US and Canadian drivers are by far the most courteous and mature, and between these extremes you will find all the rest of the world's lunatics. In Asia, if you knock someone down on the crowded roads, it is not advisable to stop. It sounds dreadful, but excitable crowds can gather at an alarming speed and the situation can get dangerously out of hand. Just drive to the nearest police station and report the accident there.

Whatever the circumstances, in an accident in Asia, it is nearly always 'the foreigner' who is blamed, and you may have to pay heavily over and above any insurance claim in 'fines', so lie in your teeth about how much money you have. (True story: while eating in a small restaurant, two overlanders saw, with dismay, a local truck smash into their parked van. The police insisted it was their fault and took their passports. Only after they'd signed a paper admitting that they had driven into the truck did they get their passports back and were allowed to go.) All you can do is be prepared for anything — and read section 11.7.3.

8.2.3. Flood

Crossing rivers under your own 'steam' should be preceded by careful reconnaissance, often on foot. Engine revs should be kept high to avoid stalling. If you do stall, water may be sucked in through the exhaust, causing extensive damage. It is often worth waiting for a local vehicle, as they usually know the best route. Slow-to-medium speed is best.

8.2.4. Damage

Some people fit stone-guards over all lights and windows. In our experience, with a laminated windscreen, this was not necessary. If your bodywork is in good shape, you can keep it that way by covering the front paintwork with a car-floor rubber sheet, cut to size, as a protection from loose chippings thrown up by passing maniacs on stony roads, such as those in Southern Argentina. Here you notice that oncoming local drivers appear to be waving to you until you realise that they hope to protect their own windscreens by pressing the tips of their splayed out fingers on the glass as they pass you. (Don't ask whether it works or not...)

All over the world, watch out for crowds of kids armed with pen-knives and an artistic urge to draw with them on your vehicle. On second thoughts ... just watch out for kids, period.

9. Paperwork

9.1. Passports

A passport can fill surprisingly rapidly. Enquire about having one with extra pages. Surrender it *only* to authorised officials when absolutely necessary (this does not mean a camp-site attendant) and store it in the safest place as mentioned in 6.9. In some instances it is possible to obtain two current passports, legally, for journeys through politically hostile countries such as in the Middle East. However, when we travelled through Africa, we did not need this, and border officials were quite prepared to stamp our entry or exit on a separate piece of paper affixed to the passport, where necessary.

9.2. Visas

Do you plan to get all your visas before departure? It will be a lot of trouble, and requires a reasonably accurate schedule which can restrict your freedom of movement. In our opinion, it is better to get them in batches from selected capitals along your route. Whichever you decide, it is worth contacting the embassies of the countries you intend to go to, so that you can get all sorts of up-to-date information.

You will need passport-size photos for most visas, and the average is two per visa. Several African countries issue a free 'transit' visa as well as the more expensive tourist ones. If you include the USA on your overland journey, it is worth getting this visa before you depart. If you apply for one outside your home country, as we did in Mexico, you will probably only be given a restricted time limit which is not extendable.

Visas do not permit you to work. Where work permits are required it will be necessary to apply for one once there, or work illegally and take the risk of deportation (without your vehicle) if caught. This aspect is covered in more detail in the next chapter.

9.3. Health certificates

The World Health Organisation and/or your local GP will tell you what certificates are necessary in the areas you intend to visit. WHO will also supply an up-to-date malaria chart. Although certificates are seldom requested at borders, it is essential that yours are in order and kept so with your six-monthly cholera jabs.

9.4. Insurance

9.4.1. Personal

Shop around for quotes for medical insurance, including Slugoki Norman, Lloyds, and ISIS on your list. Compared with the good old NHS, you will find medical facilities abroad either sadly lacking and very unhygienic, or absolutely superb and incredibly expensive. Some form of cover is definitely advisable, but don't go over the moon as you can always fly (or be flown) home if the costs are likely to get too high.

9.4.2. Vehicle

Green card insurance covers not only Europe, but extends a short way into Asia and Africa. Thereafter, third-party insurance is compulsory only in some countries. This can be obtained at borders. When it is obligatory, *don't* slip through without it — you may well meet a barrier across the road two hundred metres further on and incur a heavy fine. Sometimes it is ridiculously cheap: in India (1976) a third party policy with unlimited claims and no excess, cost us the princely sum of two US dollars for two months cover.

The insurance agent also impressed on us that, if we were about to have an accident and there was a choice between hitting a human or a farm animal, we were to be sure to hit the human, as the claim would be much cheaper for them...

A few countries will insist on a local insurance policy, *even if* you are already covered by a London company, so it is not worth trying to insure yourself for your entire trip before you leave other than a general international policy for fire and theft.

9.5. Carnet de passage

A Carnet (sometimes called a *'triptique'*) is essential. It provides exemption from the payment of local import duties for the car, for a temporary period. Should your car be sold (or stolen and therefore not re-exported within the stipulated period) the customs authorities of that country will claim the duty, plus possibly a lot more, from the organisation issuing the carnet, who in turn will get it from you. As a result, it is often necessary to put up a sizeable guarantee before you can get a carnet. The RAC or AA will tell you more, but may not necessarily be the cheapest place to get one. When you get yours, make sure the typed details are all correct, as many border officials can be extremely fussy.

Many travellers have contacted us about the difficulties of sorting out the huge deposit or guarantee that the Carnet-issuing authority requires. One solution is to take out an insurance policy which is for the amount the issuing-authority requires as indemnity, and use that as the guarantee. Then you only have the premium to pay. Slugoki Norman (see address section) is one of many Companies that can give more information.

9.6. Borders
There is usually much paperwork and an equal amount of confusion at border posts. (Our record was 5½ hours just to get *out* of Afghanistan.) Keep cool, look smart, and try to stay friendly — despite the often surly rejoinders you may receive. Your own pen, and a couple of sheets of carbon paper, may speed things up a bit. Check that all forms are filled in *accurately* both by you and the officials, as people have been known to have to return the whole distance to their point of entry to have an inaccurately filled-out form corrected. Sometimes you will be faced with a greedy little pig of an official who makes it abundantly clear that he fancies some of your whisky or a cassette or three. He knows he has the power to give you a hard time, but in our opinion it is worthwhile making a stand. However, if others succumb, it is doubly frustrating...

9.7. Driving permit
The RAC or AA can provide you with a one-year international driving permit on production of your current driving licence, some money, and a couple of photographs. Many foreign officials find the absence of any sort of number on it desperately puzzling. Typing or rubber stamping one on the front cover makes everybody happy! At several of the numerous check-posts in South America, presentation of a used library ticket proved entirely satisfactory to the soldier on duty. Nevertheless, the real thing is essential.

9.8. Student cards
There appear to be more forged student cards than ordinary ones. The former can be easily tracked down in big cities such as Athens, Bangkok, Teheran etc. If you have the genuine kind,

you may find it being questioned when you present it. Whatever kind you have, it *must* contain your photograph, and they are often useful for all kinds of price reductions.

A roadsign on the route through the Khyber Pass in Pakistan. Note the number of people paying to ride in and on the taxi!

10. Money

10.1. Budget

How long is a piece of string? How much money do I need for an overland journey? Both are unanswerable, but the following may help:

Approximately 80% of your money will go on the vehicle, so *current* fuel prices are worth finding out from a major international petrol company. Printed information will almost certainly be out of date, so beware. Try the relevant foreign embassies as well. We rarely ate out, and during the entire time, seldom paid camping fees — preferring to camp 'wild'.

The following guide should serve as a foundation to working out a reasonably accurate budget for an overland journey:

a) Allow a maximum of 400 km per day for 5 out of every 7 days. This will be a general maximum, as one day a week usually gets used up shopping, washing, repairing, maintaining etc., and at least once a week it is advisable to relax and remain stationary. There are times when you travel seven days a week, and others when you stop for several days in some idyllic corner, so it averages out at 5.

b) Calculate the *approximate* mileage of the trip; then add to your m.p.g. a good percentage for detours etc., and allocate a sum for oil/tyres and general running according to the make/age of vehicle:

c) Divide the total no. of kilometres by 400* to give the travel days, and add two for every five to give an indication of the number of weeks. Then add quite a few more to avoid belting through all those fascinating places of interest you'll hear about from other travellers you meet. Provided you are prepared to buy and cook *local* rather than imported foods bought in local markets as you go, your daily living costs are tiny compared to the running cost of the vehicle. Less than one fifth of your money will go on food, films, visas, and so on, while four fifths of the budget will go on the vehicle.

d) Decide whether time or distance is the principal factor. If you have a limited time, the distance covered will have to be regulated accordingly. If you have all the time in the world, but a limited amount of money to spend, then the slower you go and the less distance per day will give you the better value. For example, if you've let your house and will be travelling on the rent money (as many retired couples do) then when the monthly money begins to run low, all you have to do is stop for a week or so until the next lot is mailed out to you.

c) If your trip involves trans-ocean shipping, it is possible to get a very approximate guide to the cost by getting a quote from a shipping company if you supply them with the measurements of the vehicle in cubic metres and the two countries you wish to ship from/to. (*See chapter on 'Shipping'*). This cost must be added to the budget as it is the most horrifically expensive part of the trip. See also 11.7.2.

*Note: Although it is possible to do considerably more km per day in Europe or the USA where multi-lane freeways are common, you will be travelling on poor (frequently dirt) roads, clocking up low daily mileages. 400 km per day is a fair average.

10.2. Arrangements
Make arrangements to have money sent to you periodically, rather than carting large quantities with you. Always keep what you consider to be a reasonable reserve in hand for an unexpected repair or medical bill. A mixture of cash (some small and some large US dollar bills) and travel cheques (again in dollars) is the most useful combination. In some areas we found travel cheques very difficult to cash, while in others a couple of banks absolutely refused to accept cash dollars as they claimed their personnel were not able to detect forgeries.

Many banks in India (including American Express in Delhi) refused to cash a dollar bill larger than $20. Embassies are rarely helpful if you are in a spot, as they tend to view overland travellers as a pain in the diplomatic ass. Genuinely world-wide credit cards such as Diners or American Express can be useful at times, and you can always sell your blood, hair, teeth or whatever, if you are really stuck.

Before you leave have a good long chat with your bank manager, if you are on speaking terms. Although he won't be into overland travelling, he should come up with various schemes for sending money to you in Timbuctu, or Santa

Domingo de los Colorados, or wherever you wish. However, what he won't tell you is that banks abroad can get themselves into far worse tangles than they do at home. While nearly all of our many collections were relatively trouble-free ("Good morning. My name is Hewat and I have come to collect some money that is waiting for me here." Pause, and search in drawers and cupboards. "Sorry, your money has not arrived yet. Will you call back tomorrow?" Sigh. "Yes it has. It was sent at least six weeks ago." Further search, and a few telephone calls. "Yes, sir, we do have it. It was on our fourth floor, filled under 'D'.") we nevertheless did have our share of problems: One week waiting in Rwanda, six days in Chile, two weeks in Panama, a week in Iran, and ten days in Turkey. And sitting in a big city waiting for your money is no joke.

There are various precautions you can take: When *ordering* money, always send a confirmation a couple of days later. Do it well in advance if possible. Arrange that your bank automatically writes to you c/o Poste Restante at the city where you are to collect the money, confirming the details so that you have proof that you are in the right branch of the right bank in the right city. Pre-sign some blank money order forms and leave them with your manager at home. Agree a fool-proof series of code-words to cut your costs if you have to cable your manager should something go wrong. For example: Disaster = Bank claims money has not arrived, please telex them immediately. Problem = Please confirm by Poste-Restante cable when/ where money was sent. TROUBLE = Hold up on money — am moving to town mentioned. Thus — a complex cable need only read "DISASTER AND TROUBLE IN DELHI" and your money *should* be in Delhi when you arrive there. Make sure you know the correct cable and telex address to contact. Investigate the cheapest way to send money out, and consider the possibility of pre-agreeing a series of cities along your way where money can be sent well in advance, and your account *only* debited *if or when* you collect.

To impress some immigration officials, it is worth carrying a letter from your manager stating either how much you are worth (provided it's not negative!) or that you are entitled to be sent so much in any one calendar month.

Finally, there is the other possibility of giving a good and trusted friend or relative 'power of attorney'. He/she will act fast on your behalf, and won't 'close' at 5.30 or over the weekend.

10.3. Black Market
Changing money on the black market is usually very risky, but can be very profitable. For example, in East Africa in 1973, the official rate to the pound was sixteen shillings, while the black market was offering thirty five. However, things change all the time. If you decide to take the risk for a usually small profit, having checked out the situation from other travellers, please bear in mind that the black marketeer is operating illegally, cheating his country, and is just as likely to cheat you if he possibly can. He is cunning, and has many dodges up his sleeve. One transaction where you lose out will probably eliminate any profit from previous risks, and the penalty for being caught is usually instant deportation, by air and at your expense, or worse.

10.4. Reserve
There are times when nothing short of cash in either the local currency or small US dollar bills can help you. Keep a reserve entirely separate from your normal travelling cash. It needn't be more than twenty or thirty dollars, but if you do use it for some emergency, replace it as soon as possible.

10.5. Earning en route
It is possible, if you have the time, to change the flow of money from outgoing to incoming. Casual work such as fruit-picking, waitressing, petrol pump attendant etc. can be found in the richer countries, though work permits are often needed and you can be deported if found working without one. Teaching English can be very lucrative, particularly in Tokyo, and it is usually not necessary to have any academic qualifications if it is your native tongue. If you are talented, musically, there are plenty of possibilities for earning money. If not, you should use your wits.

The German mentioned at the beginning of section 6.1. travelled entirely on the proceeds of the sale of small leaflets which he got printed, locally and in the local tongue, about his adventures. If you know someone who runs a suitable shop, you can make arrangements to ship back 'gifts' of local handicrafts for them to sell. However, don't be seduced by the many tales you will hear of the small fortunes people intend to make (future tense) on the stuff they are avidly buying, once they get back home. It does not always work.

Finally, unless you are going to do something really spectacular, have a lot of strings to pull, and are extremely lucky as well, it is a complete waste of time to try to get massive sponsorship for an overland journey these days.

11. On the road

11.1. Food

Don't be tempted to haul loads of supermarket goodies with you. You will, of course, sometimes miss the huge variety of foods you are used to but, however much you take, it will run out sooner or later. If you are at all adventurous, you should enjoy food-shopping in local bazaars and experimenting with local tastes. Much fruit and veg. will be strange and unfamiliar to you, but find out about it and give it a try. Where there are people you will always find food (of sorts) and you will probably view with scorn the traveller who is still ploughing through his cans of Sainsbury's beef goulash as far away as Madras.

Fresh meat is sometimes a bit of a problem, being very gory and often dirty, but vegetarian or dairy cooking will get you by, always. The inventory (section 13) will be a guide if adapted to your tastes, especially if you follow the notes (23 to 29). Canned foods are usually expensive, but prices of fresh locally grown produce are nearly always good value if you avoid tourist areas. Be very wary of lettuce, as in poor countries it is often grown on human excrement. Apples, tomatoes etc are always safe if you peel them.

As an alternative to cooking in the van, there are always plenty of local restaurants. If you stick to European-style joints you will push up your budget fast. On the other hand, be careful about cleanliness in the local dives. Although they are usually much more interesting in terms of unusual food and clientele, while being considerably cheaper also, you run the risk of having some unhappy after-effects until your stomach becomes a bit hardened.

Crossing the Sahara or in the African jungle, it will be necessary to take two or three weeks supply of food with you. Unless you are partial to camel meat or dried monkey, you will be only too happy to open yet another packet of somewhat tasteless 'Camper's-beef-curry-for-one, -with-rice!'

11.2. Water

Drinking water for delicate Western stomachs can be a problem. Sterilising tablets are o.k. though there is often a resulting 'taste' to the water. If the budget allows it, a water-purifier is very useful in the three more primitive areas; Africa, Asia and South America.

The two most popular types are the Swiss 'Katadyn' and the Anglo-American 'Safari' range. To be effective, sterilising by boiling requires some ten minutes on the boil, and this can push up your gas consumption. Bottled drinks are usually o.k. but fresh milk, if you can get it, should be boiled unless you are really sure of it, as it is often watered down with questionable water.

Apart from deserts and, surprisingly, the African jungle, getting water will not be a problem. Garages, hotels, camp sites, private homes and so on are obvious sources, but make sure you always indicate that you want *drinking* water. Even then it cannot be guaranteed safe, as a local person's idea of drinkable water and yours are likely to differ quite a lot. In the Sahara, availability is not too problematical as all wells are marked on the Michelin maps mentioned in 5.1. However, a purifier is a very good idea. Even more so in the Congo area, as the rivers and lakes are nearly all infested with the dreaded bug bilharzia.

To beg water from a jungle village is often to ask for something that has been carried a long distance from the nearest non-stagnant river in bowls on the head. After some time on the road, you will begin to appreciate this most precious of liquids which we still take so much for granted, even though it can carry some very unpleasant diseases.

11.3. Gas Supplies

Butane, Propane (or 'mixture') is available all over the world, but the throw-away gas cartridges are a rarity, so avoid any units that rely solely on these. You do not need to carry huge supplies (*see 6.2.8.*) but, as there is no such thing as an inter-national size thread, re-filling your gas bottles can be quite an art: first, never accept a shrug of the shoulders and cries of 'impossible' at face value. If you stand around patiently, look-ing sad and helpless (and hungry, if you're a real actor) sooner or later the tough-guy at the depot or refinery which you have already taken hours to locate, will soften up and, if only to get rid of you, have a go.

Second, Camping Gaz is definitely NOT international, but neither is any other brand. So it is absolutely essential to have some sort of adaptor that converts the tiny bore of the Camping Gaz three-kilo bottle to something similar in size to the ten-kilo Calor gas size of thread. Even these size bottles differ all over the world, but with this starting point we never failed to get a refill.

When your adaptor is screwed into the inlet/outlet valve of a Camping Gaz bottle, it must have a centre part that pushes down the ball-valve. It should not be difficult to find something that will do the job from a camping or gas-supply shop.

If you are desperate, it is possible to fill a gas bottle from a larger one by gravity with a length of hosepipe, some jubilee clips, and a bit of patience. In South Africa, it is illegal to fill Camping Gaz bottles as they do not have an additional safety release valve. However, we eventually succeeded using the 'method' outlined at the beginning of this section (11.3).

11.4. Fuel
Petrol or diesel can be found everywhere there are roads, but the former can vary considerably in quality. In underdeveloped areas it is advisable not to run your tank too low, as filling stations can be few and far between. Extra capacity is not necessary except in the Sahara or other equally off-the-beaten-track areas you are unlikely to go to. (When transferring petrol from a tin or jerry can, you can avoid a mouthful of gasoline if, instead of sucking the bottom end of the pipe, you cover the aperture of the can with your hand and blow through your fingers.

If your engine's minimum octane rating is around 90, and you find your tank is very low, and the only filling station for miles has run out of Super, and the local Regular is 67 octane or thereabouts, you run the grave risk of dropping a valve and smashing a piston — as happened to us in a remote part of Brazil. Had we been carrying some cans of STP Gas Treatment, we might possibly have saved ourselves the 4 days in a work-shop and a $300 (US) bill. Low Octane fuel is not much of a problem above a thousand metres altitude, but at sea-level in countries like India, where Super is available only in main cities (Bombay, Calcutta, Delhi) and the normal petrol is often very bad, you would be advised to carry quite a few cans of STP. Allow a can per two tankfuls of petrol, and dilute it by keeping

A telephone dial in Farsi numerals in Iran will help learning the numerals 1-9 and 0.

The face of the petrol pump is reading 5 litres. The heiroglyphics on the outside relate to the large hand and read (clockwise) one litre, two litres etc. On the inner circle — for the hand — they register in fives moving clockwise. Note that the 4 of 40 (looking like a capital E) is different to the 4 on its own on the phone dial.

topping up when the tank is half-empty. You cannot get STP in India, so take it with you. We found it was the only country where we really needed it.

By the way, to expect the merry brigade at the petrol station to know what octane their petrol is, is like expecting the air-pressure gauge to work. One of the other problems is dirty fuel. Small, extra-grubby petrol stations in villages should be avoided, and make sure you are not getting a tankful of paraffin or water. Check that the numbers on the dial (if they are working) are at zero before filling, and when the performance is finally over, count your change. Fitting an additional in-line fuel filter is not a bad idea. The ones you clean yourself are best, as you are unlikely to find spare filters *en route.*

11.5. Overnight Camping

There are very few campsites outside Europe and N. America, although the India-route is not too bad. Elsewhere, there are two alternatives: 1) Camping wild (free camping) or 2) Seeking permission. Free-camping is the nicest, as you usually enjoy privacy, solitude, peace, and quiet. However, caution is needed as you are more open to attack in areas where the people are volatile ot have a reputation for being a bit unpredictable. Driving after sunset is not advisable, so you should have selected a good spot by dusk. Stopping too early means that more curious people have the chance to realise you are there. They will usually be very friendly, but have no concept of the world 'privacy'. Check out the situation from other travellers, and if you have any doubts about it, you would probably be better not to camp alone.

Countries like Turkey, Afghanistan and Colombia require a lot of caution, but you'll soon learn to pick up the vibes. In the middle of the Sahara, you have no choice, and it is a fabulous experience with the stars like jewels in the velvet blackness of an absolutely silent desert night. Elsewhere, when you camp wild, select a spot where you are not too visible from the road. Avoid blazing lights through undrawn curtains, and position the van so that, should you wish, you can make a quick getaway without a lot of maneouvering. Finally, if someone does knock on the side of the vehicle, don't open up until you are sure of their intentions. Nine times out of ten it will just be friendly locals, come to see who you are, and often bringing a small gift. However, there is just a possibility that he may have other ideas ...

Seeking permission is rarely a problem, but is not often as nice as camping wild. Police stations, airports, hospitals, petrol stations (wait till the following morning to buy petrol) and churches are good places to try. Medium-priced hotels will often oblige though they usually want token payment which is fair, specially if they throw in a shower. Several times we went to private houses that had space to park, and were, on most occasions, lucky - once we had made it clear that we were self-sufficient, *and would leave in the morning.* Cities are always a hassle, but if you eat elsewhere and get the bed made up all ready, it is not difficult to sleep in the car park of a local Hilton — with nice loos thrown in.

As you go along, you will quickly learn the art of selecting places to stop for the night. In the course of this you will find some really great places... and some rotten ones.

11.6. Mail

Receiving letters *en route* is surprisingly nice. But being free to change your route as you go is very important. So, in our opinion, it is better not to distribute a schedule to your friends for your complete journey. Ask your most reliable friend or relative to act as 'postmaster' and have your letters sent to that one address for forwarding. Then you need only let that person know what your next pick-up point will be.

All letters should have a return address on the *back* of the envelope, and the writing on the envelope kept as simple and clear as possible. Poste Restante, your Embassies/Consulates or American Express offices are the most common pick-up points, though British Embassies on the Asia route are trying to discontinue this meagre service, and can get very stroppy at times. If you plan to use Poste Restante, and collect your mail from the main post offices along your route, make sure that all envelopes are addressed as the example below:

SMITH, J.
Poste Restante
Townsville
Country

The importance of clearly addressed envelopes cannot be emphasised enough. We learned the hard way. Envelopes addressed to 'Theresa & Jonathan Hewat' or to 'Mr J. Hewat' were often filed in the T, J, or even M box instead of the H one. Even with every precaution taken, you are unlikely to receive all your mail. In our experience, the worst places were Delhi, (and most of India), Kathmandu, Sao Paulo, and Los Angeles (where they kept mail for only ten days, and filed much of it incorrectly). In Canada and the USA, Poste Restante is called 'General Delivery'. On average, Poste Restante letters are only held for about a month. In South America, Embassies are the best bet, as the postal services are generally chaotic.

If your favourite Auntie sends you a few handkerchiefs as a Christmas present, you may have to pay a lot more than they are worth just to be allowed to collect your parcel, and if she tries to send you money through the post, it will almost certainly never reach you... Outgoing mail is equally a problem: don't post films, cassettes or anything that is at all valuable from most of the countries on your route. Wait for those precious few 'safe' countries where postal services are less unreliable. You'll find out about these as you go from others. In poor countries, especially in Asia, you must always see that the stamps on your letters are cancelled in front of you; otherwise they may well be removed, re-sold, and your letter destroyed. Aerogrammes are good in this respect.

11.7. Roads

11.7.1. Surfaces

Overland driving requires additional skills to those needed under normal conditions. Know where your 'feet' (the tyres) are in relation to your driving position. On pot-holed roads, even driving slowly, it is essential to be able to choose your path very accurately if you wish to reduce the biggest car-shuddering bumps to a minimum. Many unpaved roads have a big hump down the middle, worn by truck tyres in the wet season. To protect your underneath, it is often advisable to ride two of your wheels along the hump rather than in the tracks. When stuck in sand, snow, or mud, avoid spinning your wheels in an attempt to get out, as you will only dig yourself in deeper. 2nd gear, and a bit of clutch-slip, with medium-high revs, will often work well.

Dirt roads are frequently corrugated ('washboard surface'), and if you cross the Sahara you will meet king-size ones all the time. Hour after hour. Day after day. Week after bloody week. The vibrations will chew up your heavy-duty shock absorbers and your nerves with equal voracity. There are two schools of thought on how to cope:

The 'hares' put their collective feet down on their accelerators and go as fast as they dare. The result is that the tyres 'ride' over the tops of the corrugations, producing a throbbing hum and reduced vibrations. However, there are some mini-craters or sand drifts on the track every now and then which can bring you from 70 kph to standstill in a split second. This happened to us, and we became overnight converts to the 'tortoise' school of thought. As the name implies, the tortoises take it slowly. The vibrations of the washboard surface can reduce you to tears, but apart from your shock absorbers, you should arrive intact. *This aspect of driving is covered further in section 11.7.4.*

11.7.2. Tolls
Quite a few countries operate various schemes for extracting money from passing motorists. There are tolls to cross bridges; tolls to pay for the (future) upkeep of a road; tolls to pay for the (past) upkeep of a road; ones for entering a city if you have foreign numberplates (Kathmandu); and expressway tolls. These last can usually be avoided by free roads, and are often very costly. (We had to use one to catch our ship leaving Japan, and one hard day's driving set us back $25 US in tolls). Other tolls are not usually very expensive, but should be taken into account when preparing a budget. Somewhere in the region of $8—$10 per country will probably be ample.

11.7.3. Driving habits
The maniacs on the road have been briefly mentioned in 8.2.2. However, a few general comments may smooth your passage:

a)   In many, but not all, States in the USA, you are permitted to turn right when the traffic lights are red, provided the road is clear. It is a sensible system, and keeps the traffic flowing well.

b)   Traffic lights are often ignored by drivers (and almost always by cyclists) in many parts of Asia, so treat the green light as meaning 'Go — if you dare'.

c)   In many South American countries, and especially Brazil, an *oncoming* driver will flash his left (outside) indicator as soon as he sees you. He is probably not going to turn off across you, and is more likely to be warning a vehicle behind that it is not safe to overtake.

d)   In many parts of Asia, when you start to overtake, the driver in front may switch on his offside indicator. You pull back and wait, and then try again. The same thing happens. After a few attempts you will cotton on that this is his way of telling you that it is o.k. for you to pass him. If he flashes his kerbside one, he means 'get back' behind him. Unfortunately for you, the more internationally-minded drivers do exactly the opposite, so confusion reigns.

e)   'Survival of the biggest' is one of the most common rules of the road, so unless you want to engage in a battle of nerves, move over, and don't try to play 'chicken' with anything bigger than you are. 'Moving over' will probably mean going into the ditch...

f)   Following close behind another vehicle is very dangerous in India. Although it creates a welcome passage through the dogs, cows, chickens, horses, camels, bicycles, pedestrians, ox-carts, chatting groups of people, donkeys, buffalo, schoolkids, and all other obstacles, they all tend to close back to cover the narrow road immediately after the car or bus in front has passed, with out a thought that there might possibly be a second vehicle (you) coming by.

g)   In Mexico (for example) when approaching a narrow bridge only one lane wide, with another driver heading towards you, the one that flashes his/her lights *first* has automatic priority regardless of the fact that he/she may be further away from the narrow bit. Be warned...

h)   Lastly, but by no means least, do not drive at night. It is highly dangerous, even if you have powerful spotlights, and is the quickest way to write off your car and whatever you hit — which, inevitably, will have no lights at all.

11.7.4. Difficult terrain
If you plan to go *exploring* remote areas, you will need four-wheel-drive, extra fuel capacity, plenty of food and water, sand ladders, pick-axes, shovels, and a lot of more specialised information than is given in these notes for overland travellers who stay on what are laughingly called 'roads'. However, as overlanders often venture into surprisingly remote parts without setting themselves up as an 'expedition', a few tips are worth including here:

The Sahara, or any other desert that does not have a proper road across it, is tough by any standards — both on you and your vehicle. You must be properly prepared, and never become over-confident. Most casualties occur on second trips, when people get casual and think they know it all. To cross the Sahara, there are three main routes, *none* of which requires four-wheel-drive, though it's nice if you have it. The tracks on the East side and West side are tougher going than the most commonly travelled centre (Hoggar) route through Agadés and Tamanrasset.

You follow the track of tyre-marks with the aid of a car compass and binoculars, and must be very careful never to stray out of sight of this *'piste'*. If in doubt, stop, and recce on foot, but under no circumstances should you walk out of sight of your vehicle. If you break down, stay with your car and wait for the next vehicle to come by. There are supposed to be beacons marking the track, but most of these have disappeared. They usually comprise large oil drums with a pole stuck into them, but are rarely visible, even with binoculars, beyond one kilometre's distance, due to the mirage effect of the heat. It is not strictly necessary to travel in any kind of convoy, though you often 'pal up' with other travellers you meet in an oasis town while waiting for petrol to arrive, and continue on together.

Apart from the normal overland travelling equipment for the rest of the world, you will need the following:

Extra fuel capacity: on the Hoggar (central) route you need fuel for 800 Km, being the longest distance between pickup points. Consumption goes up by somewhere around 30% due to intense heat and soft sand patches.

Extra water capacity: (*See 6.2.11*) Enough food: a supply to last for 2-3 weeks. A shovel: government surplus ex-army fold-up ones are ideal. Sand ladders: minimum two, preferably four. If you try to track them down, or have them made up at home, before you leave, they will probably cost a lot. They also may not be suitable. On the edge of the desert in some of the small towns, these things are common. There are various types, and it is worth allowing a day or two to sort yourself out in the areas where the people know all the facts. If you have them made up, don't accept the first price offered. Bargain hard. You may also find a traveller who has just come through who can advise you and, if his are not too bashed, sell you his. A car compass: nothing posh, but not a 'toy'. Two jacks: plus two strong flat

119

extra base-plates to prevent them from sinking into the sand. (1 foot square will do). A towing cable: a good strong one, preferably steel.

Although not absolutely essential, binoculars are worthwhile. If travelling with friends in a second vehicle, and if you already own a walkie-talkie set, bring it with you.

Should a fierce sandstorm appear, you will have to stop. Coat all the windward glass with thick wax to prevent it from becoming sand-blasted opaque.

Sooner or later you will become bogged down in soft sand, and will have to extricate yourself. Here are a few guidelines:

First, check whether it's better to get out backwards or forwards. There's no point in going in deeper. Then let a little air (about half) out of your tyres, making sure your footpump is working *before* you do. This will give them extra gripping area. Remove any piles of loose sand underneath the car which will inhibit easy movement. When you are ready, try and drive out with your partner pushing, but do not spin the wheels and dig yourself in deeper. If/when this fairly easy method fails, jack up both the drive wheels and place the end of a sand ladder, extending in the direction you hope to move, under each, having removed all humps of loose sand and filled up the holes your wheels have created. The second pair of ladders can extend the length of the ladder-track if you think you will need them. (If moving forward on rear-wheel-drive, place the second pair just in front of the two front wheels.) If you tie a rope to the ladders, you can drag them behind you and so avoid having to walk back to get them once you are out. When you are ready, you have only a few seconds to get up as much speed as possible on the sand ladders to give you sufficient momentum to keep going and get out. Otherwise, you will travel the length of the sand ladder and promptly sink in again. Once out, don't forget to re-inflate your tyres.

In some instances you may be able to get yourself out by scraping away the soft sand, if you are not too badly dug in, without the tedium of de-flating your tyres. If you have not had any desert-driving experience before, it is advisable to have one practice attempt somewhere near where you buy your ladders (or where you can get them modified or strengthened) before you get too deep into the desert.

There are special sand-tyres on the market, mainly for real desert exploration. They are virtually bald, and a bit like balloons. Unless you are very rich, or are going to travel *only* on sand, you can forget about them. Tyre treads are mentioned in 6.6.

As the majority of the Hoggar route is covered with sharp stones, radials, with their relatively soft 'walls' are not as satisfactory as 8-ply fine-tread conventional ones. If your VW bus is old, and you don't mind cutting away part of the wheel arches at the rear, consider making yourself an additional hub-type device that will let you bolt a spare wheel onto each of your drive wheels, thus giving you the extra grip of double rear wheels. You'll turn your bus into something not unlike a beach-buggy, but it'll not do your rear wheel bearings much good if used for long.

In a sandstorm, there is little you can do but stop and sit it out. It may last a few hours or a few days. Do not try to keep driving as, if you lose the track, you are in serious trouble. Equally, for the same reason, *never* drive after the sun has set. You will cover the greatest distance, and keep cooler if you get up and have breakfast before sunrise, being ready to move as soon as the sun appears. Desert nights can be extremely chilly.

I can recall one evening when we had been travelling in the Sahara for over two weeks and I was beginning to get signs of the dreaded disease called 'over-confidence'. It was nearly time to stop for the night when we came to a cairn of stones on a small smooth hump near to the track. I decided to stop there for the night and drove over to the hump and up onto it. (You get familiar with the appearance of the desert after a while, and can often *see* whether the ground is firm enough for the vehicle's weight. It was.)

Being in a good mood, and having only become bogged down a few times that day, I drove round and round the stone cairn a few times before stopping.

The next morning, when I awoke, I could not tell which way we'd come, and which way we should go (had I not had a compass) as I'd chewed up my tracks by idiotically charging round and round in circles.

To judge by the sun, too, is not always infallible, as the South-bound track sometimes weaves North/East/West around the huge 'ergs' (dunes).

It was momentarily unnerving, and it reminded me that one NEVER fools around in such a potentially dangerous place as the Sahara.

In Algeria it is necessary to report in to the police at each oasis town, and give your E.T.A. for the next. This is so that they can send out a search party to look for you if you fail to arrive... in theory. In Niger, where the desert is much tougher, there is no provision for such an event. You're on your own, baby!

If you do break down, irreparably, in the middle of a desert, never leave the vehicle and try to walk. Stay with it and hope that something will come along to rescue you... soon. One way of attracting attention to your plight is to pour some fuel on your most worn tyre and set light to it. The thick column of dense black smoke rising into the sky might just attract the attention of some passing nomads, or even an aircraft.

An excellent book *'Sahara Handbook'* by Simon and Jan Glen, can be obtained from Roger Lascelles (*address in section 15*).

Jungle roads do not require the extra equipment needed for a desert crossing, and there are usually plenty of people about if you get really stuck. Snow chains, a good machete (bought locally) and the inevitable towing cable are advisable. Bamboo can frequently fall across the track and, unless you have the patience to burn it back, your machete, or an axe, will prove invaluable. The large boulders and the troughs cut by rushing water even after a very brief cloudburst make the going very slow and quite difficult at times. The bridges are often incredibly rickety and appear entirely unsafe. (Road-sign in the Congo: 'DANGER. BRIDGE IN OPERATION'.)

Ferries, which are usually free, seem equally unsafe, and often need a bit of help from you in the form of some cigarettes or a few aspirin tablets before the operator will get off his butt. Your battery, or sometimes two, may also be needed to start the motor of the more luxurious rafts...

In South America, you do not need any special equipment unless you plan to venture way off the beaten track. Probably the worst roads are in Southern Bolivia. These are sometimes made impassable in heavy rains.

11.8. Garages
A visit to a garage, even a fully authorised official workshop, is likely to be an experience not easily forgotten in a hurry. We know. We had to have our engine removed no less than nine times, often to put right what the previous bunch had done, or put back, wrong. If there is anything major to be done, be prepared to sleep a night or two in these hell-holes. It is absolutely essential to stay with your vehicle all the time, both to watch for light fingers and incompetent mechanics: a noisy, tedious, boring, and nerve-shattering experience. Spare parts are often not available, or are costly to a hideous degree, and the authorised agents are *always* the most expensive place in town. Although there is some come-back with official dealers while you are in the area, to try to claim on guarantees from one country to another is well-nigh impossible. (At one stage in our journey, after four days inside the VW garage, we emerged into the sunlight with an extra 100 cc capacity, four Ford pistons, a Mercedes valve, the distributor 180 degrees out of alignment, two plug leads crossed, and $300 the poorer! However, the mechanics were a friendly crowd, if nothing else, and gave us a concert on a motley assortment of guitars before waving farewell to us.) On a more serious note, it is worth knowing that VW sometimes operate a 'time-unit' system, whereby each job is allocated a certain number of time-units. This number, multiplied by the *local* labour charge, plus parts, should be all that you are charged, regardless of how long the job actually takes.

11.9. Pest control
Insects, whether flying, crawling or both, can be a nightmare. If you park in one spot for more than a few days, an invasion of ants or cockroaches is not funny if it gets out of hand. Avoid parking with the branch of a tree (especially palm) touching the vehicle and making a 'gangway' for columns of the little darlings. A ring of insect powder around each wheel can help, but no matter how bug-proof or mosquito-proof you believe you are, the buggers will get in somehow, sometime, somewhere. Although aerosol sprays are not always available, you can always find the old hand-pump kind.

11.10. Diary
Keeping a 'log' of the journey is a common practice among overlanders. Apart from noting impressions, events, and so on — which you're either into or you're not — consider keeping factual notes on some or all of the following: Daily and border-to-border distances. Overnight place names. Fuel consumption

(litres). Oil consumption/changes. Mechanical notes. Punctures and tyre data. Money (exchange rates, income and expenditure, dates, etc.) Photography notes (subjects, places, dates, film numbers). 'Renewals' list: carnet/insurance/injections etc. You will sometimes find this a real drag but, as memories merge or fade, its value increases.

12. Shipping

N.B. 'Shipping' in this section refers only to freighting, and does not include roll-on, roll-off ferries.

12.1. Costs

Astronomical, however you look at it! Some shipping lines charge by weight, but most go by volume, so the size of your vehicle is important. The whole process is rife with problems and is the worst part of any overland trip. If you try to sell the van instead of shipping it, and buy another one at the other side you will have equal hassles with carnet rules and regulations, and fitting out another vehicle as a home-on-wheels is likely to be difficult except in the USA or in Australia, where camping is an industry on its own. Overland travellers still turn to Europe as the best source for all equipment and information, as North American vehicles tend to be ridiculously large and luxurious for these purposes.

As shipping prices seem to rise monthly, beware of printed price lists — if you can even find them. The apparently endless trail of bureaucracy and mis-information you will encounter is enough to make anyone despair. Don't. Just bear in mind the inevitable fact that the only really reliable prices are those obtained from the agents once you have arrived at the port of embarkation, and the days when you could find a small 'tramp' steamer that would take you and your car for peanuts are over.

Beware of shipping a vehicle into Brazil. Apart from the unbelievable landing formalities, the Brazilian port charges can be utterly ruinous. No one advised us of this, if they knew about it, in Cape Town and it was only by chance we booked to Buenos Aires. Uruguay is also meant to be o.k. compared to Brazil, but check this out thoroughly.

Wherever you land your car, you will find that there are many hidden 'extras' such as landing, port, and unloading charges. (We averaged around $100 per shipping on top of the actual freight costs). If you travel with your car, it can be classed as 'accompanied baggage', which somewhat reduces the bureaucracy etc on arrival.

Travellers intending to visit South America tend to have the un-avoidable problems of shipping costs which deters only the faint-hearted (or very poor). There are three choices for Europeans or Australians:

a) Pay up and ship the vehicle there

b) Fly to the US and buy a vehicle and drive it most of the way. (All the way once the Darien Gap is opened between Panama and N. Colombia.)

c) Fly direct to S. America, and buy a vehicle there. As camping is still very much in its infancy in that part of the world, it might be advisable to bring basic equipment such as a cooker and other living equipment with you, and fit them on arrival rather than hope to find them there. Brazil and Argentina are the most likely countries to start from — with the former being ideal for buying a VW van. Having completed the trip, the vehicle could be worth more than it originally cost, having been fitted out as a camper. The disadvantages of this are that one's Spanish would have to be reasonably good at the outset, and it would almost certainly require a circular trip ending up in the country where the vehicle was bought in order to sell it again. There is also the problem of getting a *carnet* for a vehicle once you had bought it.

d) Fly to S. America, and hire a van for the length of time you intend to travel, living rough in it.

12.2. Papers
Port authorities love their paperwork as much as you will loathe it. On one occasion, we trudged around collecting the grand total of 35 separate rubber stamps on our papers over a 2½ day period before we could collect our van. Apart from wanting your money, the agent will need the vehicle's size in cubic feet/metres and weight (in kilos/tons). By dis-counting the easily removable parts such as front-mounted spare tyre, both bumpers, roof-rack etc., you may be able to squeeze the car into the next size category down and save some money. However, don't actually remove these items unless it is demanded.

Note: Even if you do not need to have a visa for (say) Argentina, and you intend to ship the vehicle there, it is worth getting what they call a 'Transit Visa' which allows you only a few days in the Country. This dramatically reduces the bureaucratic hassles at the port of arrival, and you can then drive to the nearest border (Uruguay) and *re-enter* the Country by road, automatically getting the 90-day tourist visa. A friend of ours has now done this (successfuly) three times.

Insuring the vehicle for the sea journey is either ridiculously expensive, or impossible. If you do insure, it is on the cards that you'll end up in the middle with the shipping line and the port authority each claiming it was the other's area of responsibility. Sometimes the agents tell you that the vehicle must be completely empty, and all your belongings crated and sent separately. Our advice is to say nothing if told this, and ignore it. (Officially, you have already sent your stuff by surface mail or some way that is only your business.) This apparently nonsensical rule, we were told, was so that in the event of the ship sinking and a claim being made, it would be a lot cheaper than if the car was full of all kinds of very precious belongings. Consequently, your bill of lading will probably itemise the cargo as 'one unpacked *empty* vehicle'. Nevertheless, although you are taking a risk in the event of any accident, you will save yourself the incredible task of unpacking and crating everything, plus the cost. (*See 12.6.*)

12.3. Timing

Freighters usually run late, and are somtimes re-scheduled at the last moment, by the owners. They can miss your port entirely, or change cargo so that it becomes possible to take your vehicle. In these instances, the agent will do his best to re-accommodate you. This can, however, work to your advantage as well because, once you've arrived at the port you may find a ship that can take you at very short notice. One of the most reliable sources of information on shipping lines and schedules is the *ABC Shipping Guide*. It is regularly updated. Ask someone in Thos. Cook's travel agencies to let you have a browse through theirs in a quiet period. They may even give you a recently out-of-date copy. If you try to pre-book your shipping before you set off, you'll encounter such a welter of unreliable information that you may be tempted to give up. Don't be discouraged. Try to be flexible and play as much of your trip as possible by ear.

12.4. Damage

You are most likely to incur damage when shipping the van. Apart from the rough handling on the docks, keep a wary eye out for rubbing ropes and cables when it is being lifted or lashed down. *Stick to your car like glue,* and let the mob see that you care about its treatment. They will respond to this surprisingly well if your approach is friendly rather than arrogant. And if you take the trouble to polish the paintwork (or at least wash it fairly thoroughly) beforehand, it will get a lot more respect than that filthy-looking rusty old hippy-wagon beside you.

12.5. On-deck protection

Make the effort to get your van shipped *below* decks if possible, as salt air can wreak havoc in a very short time. If you fail, cover the car with some form of tarpaulin. These may not be forthcoming from the agent or the crew, and you may have to buy some plastic sheeting. It's worth it, except on the MV Chidambaram (Malaysia-India route) where the ship is so large that the spray is very unlikely to come up and over, and the voyage is only four days. However, it is advisable to wash the van thoroughly on arrival.

12.6. Thieves

Thieves abound in profusion at all docks. Stay with your vehicle the entire time, *day and night.* If you ignore this advice, almost certainly something(s) will be stolen. The agent may tell you to deliver the car to the docks a couple of days before it is due to be loaded. Try and avoid this. Docks are not the loveliest of places to camp in. If told that you can't sleep in your car on the docks, either insist on taking it away, or pass the buck onto the authorities by seeing that it is locked into a bonded warehouse.

If you are shipping your van with all your belongings in it, the following advice should prove helpful:

a)   **Remove** everything 'removable' from the exterior. Horns, hubcaps, wipers, wing mirrors etc. If you don't, someone else will.

b) **Seal** the living area from the driving cab. If your bus is a walk-through version, this may mean making a template from newspaper, and getting a sheet of ply jig-saw cut as a partition which can be discarded on arrival. It's worth the effort, as it would take time to break down.

c) **Draw** all curtains in the living area so that no one can see in.

d) **Remove** everything from the driver's cab. (Mirrors, fan, cassette player, ashtray, compass, contents of glove compartment etc).

e) **Double-lock** living area doors, having padlocked all interior cupboards.

f) **Pray**.

Once at sea, if the above precautions have been taken, you can relax... as you talk to your Maker on the great white telephone — until you've got your sea-legs.

All this may sound excessive. It isn't. During our entire journey we did not meet a single traveller who had not had something stolen — usually while shipping. We lost only an air-horn, as we stupidly forgot to remove it on one occasion.

If you have a steering lock, you may have to leave the key in the ignition. Make sure that it cannot be used to open any living area doors. The petrol tank will have to be almost empty, and as the battery must be disconnected, your burglar-alarm will not work.

Leather Craftsman laughing at some incomprehensible joke (probably about us) when we collected some superb and inexpensive handmade boots in Herat (Afghanistan)

13. Inventory (2 people + van, except 13.8.)

This section should really have been called 'Inventory for *comfortable* travelling'. It is not a complete list of what to take, as only you can decide that, but it may help as a check-list for planning.

If you use it to prepare your *own* list and then cut out around 40%, you will be on the right lines for a comfortable and uncluttered journey. However, you will have to be very tough with yourself, as ignorance of what it is like 'out there' often scares beginners into taking the whole lot with them — until they learn... Basing this inventory on our own experiences, each item has been categorised into one of the following three groups:

(a) Either essential, or highly recommended
(b) Advisable, but not essential
(c) Not necessary — but included for consideration

On the premise that you intend to travel in comfort (but not luxury), those items marked (a) are what we think is a basic minimum. Many travel with much less, but not very comfortably. Group (b) depends more on your budget and the route you plan to take, and should be adapted accordingly. Use Group (c) as a reminder-list for your own individual requirements — but be very restrictive.

The recommended quantities are printed in brackets. For example, (1+3) indicates a running stock of three, with one in use. Where no quantity is mentioned, it is either singular or obvious. *The 'superior' numbers refer to the Notes in 13.10.*

Finally, when reading this inventory, please remember:

1) It is included only as a guide.
2) Every ounce of weight should justify its inclusion.
3) You are always near to people, and that means food, water, clothes etc.
4) Improvisation is always possible.
5) If in doubt, *leave it out!*

13.1. *Furniture*

Water bottles & pipe[1](a)
Water pump[2] (a)
Purifier or tablets (a)
Sink + toothbrush hldr (a)
Bed[3] (a)
Cushions/pillows 2(a)
Seatcovers, *see 6.2.2.* (b)
All-round curtains (a)
Gas bottles + regulators (a)
Cooker (a)
Small garbage bin + lid (a)
Table[4] (a)
Fold-up chairs (2) (b)
Fire Extinguishers (2) (a)
Fridge[5] + Brush[6] (b)
Mosquito netting (a)
Roof vent (b)
Louvre windows (b)
Electric fan(s) (b)
Interior sockets/plugs (b)
Int. lights + spares (b)
Radio/tape + spkrs[7] (b)
Heater[8] (c)
Seat belts (a)
Headrests (safety) (b)
Car compass (a)
Interior anti-crash bar (c)
Portable toilet (c)
Tarpaulin (c)
Canopy, *see 6.2.18* (b)
Tent equipment (c)
General purpose mirror (b)
Second rear-view mirror (c)
Writing paper etc (b)

13.2 *Mechanical & upkeep*

Tool box + basic tools[9] (a)
Box of spare parts[10] (a)
Footpump (a)
Wheelbrace (a)
Pair of tyre irons (b)
Jacks + base plates (a)
Spare wheels & tubes (a)
Puncture kit, *see 6.6.* (a)
Snow chains (c)
Strong towing cable (a)
Jerry cans, *see 11.4.* (b)
Fuel filter *see 11.4.* (c)
Locking petrol cap (a)
Cans of STP, *see 11.4.* (c)
General purpose funnel (c)
Grease gun & grease (b)
Spare engine oil can (b)
2 batteries + switches (a)
Extra horn & button[11] (c)
Voltage converter[12] (c)
Small inspection light (c)
Small hand-drill + bits (c)
Breakdown triangle[13] (a)
Gas spares[14] + adaptor[15] (a)
Flexible sealant (2 tubes) (b)
Glycerine[16] (c)
Window/car cleaning kit (c)
Anti-freeze for screen (b)
Anti-rust paint + brush (c)
Touch-up paint (c)[17]
Compact shovel (a)
Small axe or machete (c)
Tape head-cleaning kit (b)

13.3. *Kitchen*

Plates (4 lge, 2 sml) (a)
Bowls (2 cereal) (a)
Egg cups (2) (a)
Unbreakable glasses[18] (a)
Cutlery (4 of each) (a)
Kitchen scissors (b)
Potato peeler (b)
Tin opener/corkscrew (a)
Knife sharpener (b)
Kitchen knife (a)
Bread/chopping board (b)
Kettle (a)
Pans/pressure cooker (a)
Non-stick frying pan (b)
Boiling pan (clothes) (b)
Spatulas (2) (a)
Pan scourers (1+6) (a)
Washing up liquid (1+1) (a)
Cleaning powder (1+1) (a)
Plastic washing up bowl (a)
Dishcloths (1+1) (a)
Tea towels (1+2) (a)
Garlic press (c)
Citrus fruit squeezer (b)
Rough/fine cheese grater (b)
Plastic egg box (b)
Airtight boxes[19] (b)
Butter/margarine box (b)
Salt/pepper pots (b)
Black pepper grinder (c)
Sieve/strainer (b)
Teapot (a) and Strainer (b)
Small (gen purpose) jug (c)
Sugar jar for table (b)
Muslin coffee filter[20] (b)
Thermos flask (c)
Barbeque equipment[21] (c)
Mini petrol stove[22] (c)
Silver foil (1+1) (b)
Marble[5] (1 + 1)(b)

13.4. *Food Stocks*

Coffee (instant/real)[23] (a)
Tea (½ kilo) (a)
Salt (1 pkt) (a)
Pepper (white & black) (b)
Dried milk[24] (a)
Canned milk (2-3 tins) (b)
Sugar (3 kilos) (a)
Mustard (1 small tin) (c)
Vinegar (1 bottle) (b)
Lemon Juice[25] (a)
Conc. fruit squash (1+1) (b)
Various fresh fruit/veg (a)
Sultanas/raisins etc (c)
Bread (a)
Dry biscuits[26] (2 pkts) (b)
Mayonnaise[27] (c)
Bovril/Marmite (1 big jar) (a)
Beef/chicken stock[28] (a)
Jam/marmalade (1 pot) (b)
Curry powder (1 pkt) (b)
Assorted spices/sauces (b)
Tinned foods[29] (a)
Fresh marge/butter (1 pkt) (a)
Marge/butter (2 sml tins) (a)
Tomato paste (6 v sml tins) (a)
Flour (1 kilo) (a)
Rice (1 - 2 kilos) (a)
Yeast (1 tin, *see 6.2.9.*) (b)
Spaghetti (1 - 2 pkts) (b)
Cooking oil (1 litre) (a)

13.5. *Day-to-day*

Face flannels (2) (a)
Hand towels (3 medium) (a)
Soap (1 + 1) & container (a)
Toothbrushes (2) (a)
Nailbrush (b)
Nail scissors (b)
Haircutting scissors (b)
Hairbrush/combs (a)
Shampoo (1 + 1) (a)
Shaver kit[30] (c)
Tissues (2 boxes) (b)
Toilet paper (1 + 3) (a)
Hot water bottle (b)
Good sleeping bags (2) (a)
Liners for above[31] (2 prs) (a)
Pillowcases (4) (a)
Contraceptives, *see 7.3.* (a)
Tampax, *see 7.3.* (a)
Safety pins (b)
Detergent (1 + 1 med boxes) (a)
Dustpan & brush (a)
Sewing kit (a)
Assorted rubber bands (c)
Glue (1 tube) (c)
String (1 ball) (b)
Masking tape (1 roll) (b)
Sellotape (1 roll) (b)
Pens/pencils/erasers (b)
Lighter/matches (a)
Living area ashtray (c)
Mosquito coils (2 boxes)[32] (b)
Insect spray (1 + 1) (a)
Insect powder (2 pkts) (b)
Flashlight (a good one) (a)
Spare torch batteries (c)
Umbrella (share one?) (b)
Sunglasses (2 + 1) (a)
Suntan oil (2 bottles) (b)
Lip salve (1) (c)
Swiss Army penknife (a)
Binoculars (b)
Handbag/purse/shopping bag (a)
Minimal make-up kit (b)

13.6. *Medical etc*

Basic first aid kit (a)
Lomotil (runs) (50 tabs) (a)
Bites/stings cream (a)
Malaria tablets (a)
Salt tablets (app 50) (b)
Disp. needles, *see 7.1.* (a)
Disinfectant (1 bottle) (a)
Toothache 'cure', *see 7.1.* (a)

13.7. *Papers and leisure*

Passports (a)
Supply of visa photos (a)
Vaccination certs (a)
Driving licences (GB) (b)
International licences (a)
Carnet de passage (a)
Vehicle log book (a)
Insurance certs, *see 9.4.* (a)
Diary (b)
Calendar (c)
Cookery book (c)
First aid manual (a)
Workshop manual (a)
Guide/reference books (b)
English dictionary (b)
Foreign dictionaries (b)
Paperback books (10-12) (b)
Address book (a)
Compendium of games [33] (c)
Student cards (b)
Selected maps (a)
Portable Typewriter (c)
Photo equipment (b)
Films & lens cleaner (b)
Spare light-mtr battery (b)
Cassette storage box (c)
Headphones [34] (c)
Flippers/mask/snorkel/ (c)
Lilo airbed (c)
Fold-up rucksacks [35] (2) (c)
Fishing equipment (c)

13.8. *Clothes (per person)*

Flip-flops or sandals (a)
Walking shoes (a)
Hiking boots (b)
Wellingtons (share?) (b)
Socks (3-4 pairs) (a)
Underwear (3-4 sets) (a)
Night clothes (c)
Jeans (2-3 pairs) (a)
Shorts (1 pair) (a)
Belt (money belt?) (a)
Skirt (2, one long) (a)
Shirts/blouses (3-4) (a)
T-shirts (3-4) (a)
Swimming suit (1) (a)
Sunhat (1 small) (b)
Jacket or short coat (b)
Warm jumpers (2) (b)
Jump suit [36] (c)
Gloves (1 pair) (b)
Fold-up raincoat (a)
Posh clobber [37] (b)

13.9. *Miscellaneous*

Anti-fog spray (2-3) (c)
Carbon paper (2 shts) (c)
Clothes line & pegs (a)
Shoe cleaning kit (b)
Sets of spare keys (2) (a)
Padlocks, as necessary (a)
Travel (alarm) clock (b)
Flat rubber disc [38] (b)
Various small gifts (c)
Weapons, *see 8.1.* (c)
Strobe timing light [39] (c)
Candles (1 box) (c)
Altimeter (c)
Thermometer (c)
Fold-up suitcase [40] (c)
Briefcase (see Note 37) (c)
This book...

13.10. Notes
The following notes relate to the 'superior' numbers set in the text of the inventory on the previous pages.

Note 1   Three or four ten-litre containers should be ideal for a normal overland journey.   However, a couple of *collapsible* additional ones can be very useful on wash-day, or for long stop-overs on a beach where sweet water is scarce.   Sahara crossings, or other really remote areas, require a larger total capacity although, on our journey, we *never* carried more than 70 litres which, with a water purifier, gave us the possibility of re-cycling water in a dire emergency.   A 1-metre length of hose-pipe with a tap fitting can be very useful when the gap between sink and tap is too small to fit your bottles into, and no other tap is available.

Note 2.   Manual or foot-operated ones are usually more sturdy than electric ones.   If you have an electric one, take some spares.

Note 3.   It is worth making some removable, washable, seat-cushion covers. The cushions get heavy wear as they usually double as a mattress for the bed.

Note 4.   If the table is 'clip-on' (*see 6.2.3.*) it is worth having four screw-on legs so that it can be set up outside as well.

Note 5.   In very hot weather, a heat-exchange operated fridge is hard put to do its job.   When parked, the more level it is, the better it will work, so a small spirit level (or even a marble) is useful to take with you.

Note 6.   Some gas can be very poor quality, creating a lot of soot in the fridge chimney.   A bottle-brush, or similar, is useful.

Note 7.   Four speakers are worth the effort.   You won't hear much music to your taste until you get back home again other than what you bring with you.   The radio aerial must be mounted well out of reach of idle passers-by and small boys.

Note 8.   Bulky, free-standing heaters take excessive space (and are useless in hot climates). Track down a small one which you can build in, if possible.   Gas operated ones are best from the fuel availability point of view.   Make sure you place it in a safe position.

Note 9. Include the following: Spanners (open/ring/socket), screw-driver set (small/large/Phillips), pliers/cutters, Mole grips, hammer, assorted wire, spark-plug-remover, sandpaper, Gungum or Firegum, oil, penetrating oil, hand (metal) saw, feeler-gauge, tyre pressure gauge, assorted nuts/bolts/screws/hooks/hinges/washers etc, small file, Allan keys, insulating tape, assorted Jubilee clips, and from there on, whatever you feel you will use, depending on your mechanical ability.

Note 10. The choice is up to you, but consider the following: Heavy duty shock absorbers, points (several), plugs (ditto), fan belt, brake fluid and bleeding kit, oil filters (several) assorted bulbs, fuses, distributor cap, rotor arm, HT and spark-plug lead, various gaskets, fuel pump kit, accelerator cable, clutch cable, brake cable, brake pads/shoes, wiper blades, fold-up plastic windscreen... If you start into the pistons, rings, valves and grinding paste bit, you are a good mechanic (and don't need this note anyway) or you are in danger of taking too much stuff with you.

Note 11. Not necessary *unless* India is on your route. Then, the louder the better, with the passenger doing the hooting!

Note 12. A small unit is available that converts 12v to a choice of 6v, 7.5v, or 9v current. If you take a portable radio or tape recorder, it will pay for itself on the savings in the usually high price of torch batteries. Make sure that the radio/recorder has a suitable external input socket.

Note 13. Compulsory in several countries, particularly Europe.

Note 14. Some spare rubber gas-pipe, a 'Y' joint, an in-line on/off tap, suitable Jubilee clips, a roll of thread-sealing tape, and a spare jet for the refrigerator.

Note 15. A really essential item for remoter parts. Most refineries/depots do not have connections that go as small as the thread on Camping Gaz bottles. You will need an adaptor that allows them to connect to your bottles via larger thread junctions similar to the threads on the ten-kilo size of Calor gas bottles. Once you are that sort of size, miracles can be worked. The sort of adapter required is shown on p87. Note that where it screws into the Camping Gaz bottle, it must push the ball-valve down to allow the gas to enter.

Note 16. Every few months, it is advisable to wipe some glycerine over all rubber sealing strips around the windows to prevent perishing in extremes of weather.

Note 17. Vehicle colours are often national rather than international. Touch-up paint in your colour may not exist abroad.

Note 18. From our experience, we found glasses much more pleasant to drink from than either plastic or enamel. The unbreakable variety of heat-resistant glasses with plastic holders are ideal. Even if they won't break, they can disappear, so take a couple of extra spares with you.

Note 19. These are very useful (assorted sizes) for storing tea, sugar, rice, flour, dried fruits etc. They are also insect-proof. (Yes you'll have a few cockroaches in the van. Ugh!)

Note 20. Instant coffee is usually more expensive than beans. The shop will grind them for you, but you'll need a cup-filter. Forget paper-filter devices as you often won't find the paper filters. A muslin bag on a wire or plastic ring, that sits on the cup will last you the whole trip.

Note 21. Open-fire cooking is often possible, enjoyable, and cheap. You can assemble a suitable 'rack' from a household chrome-plated plate-rack with four sturdy clip-on legs. Don't take 'Sunday Times' type of barbecue equipment. A flat metal plate (like a 'Wimpy' frier) is also good for frying eggs etc.

Note 22. The Swedish 'Optimus' brand, available in Britain, is excellent. Unless you are diesel-powered, you carry the fuel with you anyway. It can save gas, and is useful if you plan to leave the vehicle and go off hiking.

Note 23. It is worth taking a very large tin of instant coffee with you, as it is likely to be nearly double the price in many countries. Also, if you are at all sociable, you may enjoy inviting others into your van for an evening cup of coffee and an exchange of information about the area or roads.

Note 24. Dried/powdered milk is available everywhere, but it often requires great skill to mix to avoid lumps, unlike the home varieties. Therefore, as it is light and compact, it is worth setting off with a reasonably large quantity. Fresh milk is rarely pasteurised (when you can get it) and should be boiled on most occasions. Some milk is watered down with questionable water, also. Canned milk is always available and o.k. as an alternative.

Note 25. When in a country where fresh lemons are cheap, buy and squeeze loads, as the juice can be kept in airtight bottles. Mixed with sugar and water, it makes a very refreshing drink.

Note 26. When bread is difficult to track down, you can make your own (*see 6.2.9.*) or turn to your stock of dry biscuits.

Note 27. Or make your own: oil (preferably olive) plus lemon juice (see note 25, above) and a pinch of mustard, salt, pepper and thyme, whisked together thoroughly and poured over the salad at the last moment. Beware of lettuce in poor/dirty countries and always peel tomatoes. (*see 11.1.*)

Note 28. Get hold of a large jar of each. Cubes are a more costly way of buying and, if you plan ahead, your favourite local restaurant will probably do you a favour and get you these from their bulk-buying source. Along with Bovril and Marmite, one of the most useful things for 'tasty' cooking.

Note 29. A small selection of versatile tinned foods is worth taking. A dozen should be ample, if used more as stand-by resources in more sparse areas. Tuna, minced meat and such like are the most useful, as you can use them as bases to 'do things with'.

Note 30. If you don't like shaving 'wet' and don't intend to grow a beard, you can buy a small booster unit that converts 12v to 110/220v, but it is for shavers only.

Note 31. Considerably easier to keep clean than sleeping bags.

Note 32. Wherever there are mosquitoes you can get these coils. If you light them early enough in the evening, they will allow you to cook with doors and windows open without being eaten alive.

Note 33. Cards, scrabble, chess, backgammon, draughts, or whatever.

Note 34. Surprisingly useful — if you already own a set. You will need to rig up something to plug the 'jack' into. Avoid driving with these on as, apart from being dangerous, you'll need to keep an ear open for strange engine noises. If one of you wants music and the other doesn't, they are ideal.

Note 35. There is a plastic rucksack on the market that folds into one of its pockets and ends up about 7" x 4" x 2". When open it will hold two sleeping bags plus oddments. They are not very tough, but useful for the odd hiking trip.

Note 36. Something like a track suit. If you are going to be in very cold weather, they can be worn with gloves and socks both by day and in bed at night.

Note 37.   It is not a bad idea to have one outfit that won't get you thrown out of a half-respectable restaurant or hotel for the odd night out on the town.   You can leave the tiara and pearls behind, and *one* outfit per person should be enough.   If possible, it should be one that can double for both day and evening use — especially if there is a chance you might work for a short time *en route*.   A briefcase could be useful if you work, and can be used to store maps etc if not.

Note 38.   When you are lucky enough to track down a sink with running water to do the washing in, it is almost guaranteed not to have a plug.   A flat rubber disc that will cover the largest plug hole will be a blessing.

Note 39.   This is quite useful if you know how to use it.   Most overlanders use the old alligator clip device (home-made) to time the engine, but it is not nearly as accurate.   Many of the more modern engines *must* be timed by strobe.   You should know how to time the engine correctly.   Many workshop mechanics are not up to such simple procedures.   Know why you do what you do as well as how to do it.

Note 40.   If you stay with your vehicle all the time you won't need one.   If you have the rucksacks (*see note 35, above*) you also probably won't need one.   But if you plan to spend some nights in the odd hotel — even just for the luxury of a hot bath — it could be useful.   The soft, fold-up ones are best.

14. Statistics

The following section of statistical information is a collection of facts related to our particular journey. Much of it is useless, but we decided to include it as a possible aid to planning and budgeting a journey of your own. Like statistics of all kinds, they do not prove anything...

When we left England in January 1973, the pound sterling was worth 2.35 US dollars. By the time we returned, about 3½ years later, it was worth 1.76 dollars. When we were in Japan (from March to August 1975) cantaloupe melons were selling at the amazing price of 3,000 yen, or $10.38 each. On the other hand in Cameroons, in March 1973, we bought an enormous pineapple which weighed 5 kilos, for only the equivalent of 10p. So the horrific usually balances out with the good in one way or another as we found out when, having paid $115 for the supply and fitting of a new ignition switch and harness in L.A., U.S.A., we had to have exactly the same job done again in Bangkok, Thailand, by the chief VW mechanic, one Saturday afternoon. The price? Two cups of coffee, a half bottle of awful Japanese whisky, and eight U.S. dollars for the parts!

14.1. Distances

Total distance of journey	143,305 km
Europe: (2,816 at beginning & 6,190 at end)	9,225 km
Africa: (7 February to 3 December 1973)	34,580 km
S. America: (21 December '73 to 22 July '74)	34,178 km
C. and N. America: (23 July '74 to 13 Mar '75)	35,940 km
Japan: (28 march to 29 August 1975)	7,034 km
Malaya peninsula: (9 September to 29 Oct 1975)	6,834 km
Remainder of Asia: (2 Nov '75 to 14 Apr '76)	15,514 km
Greatest distance covered in one day (U.S.A.):	667 km
Shortest distance (8½ hrs driving, E. Zaire):	66 km
Longest distance between fuel and water pick-up points (Niger, Southern Sahara).	800 km

The 'shortest distance' included a break for lunch of about an hour, but mainly involved battling with mud, boulders etc.

14.2. Speeds

Usual cruising speed:	85 kph	(on paved roads)
Maximum cruising speed	118 kph	(on paved roads)

14.3. Countries
The following list gives the countries we visited. These are in approximate order as we sometimes entered a country more than once. The numbers represent the number of days spent in that particular country. (Sea-crossings are not included.) Of the 56 countries visited, and over 120 border-crossings, only two bothered to search the van thoroughly: Chile & Afghanistan.

France, 8. Spain, 5. Morocco, 6. Algeria, 17. Niger, 7. Nigeria, 13. Cameroons, 6. Central African Republic, 5. Zaire, 23. Rawanda, 10. Kenya, 36. Tanzania, 16. Malawi, 14. Zambia, 6. Botswana, 2. Rhodesia, 25. South Africa, 105. Swaziland, 2. Lesotho, 2. SW Africa, 5. Argentina, 51. Uruguay, 3. Brazil, 40. Paraguay, 15. Chile, 29. Peru, 37. Bolivia, 19. Ecuador, 16. Colombia, 13. Panama, 15. Costa Rica, 2. Nicaragua, 2. Honduras, 1. El Salvador, 2. Guatemala, 5. Belize, 3. Mexico, 26. United States, 161. Canada, 21. Japan, 155. Singapore, 8. Malaysia, 18. Thailand, 24. India, 83. Nepal, 8. Pakistan, 30. Afghanistan, 17. Iran, 24. Turkey, 17. Greece, 24. Jugoslavia, 9. Austria, 1. Germany, 6. Netherlands, 1. Belgium, 2. and France (again), 1.

14.4. Fuel
Total petrol consumption (London to London):   20,417 litres
Average petrol consumption (approx. 20 mpg):   6.95 kpl
Most expensive petrol (Central Africa, 1973):   92c(U.S.) a litre
Cheapest petrol (S.American Andean countries): 6c(U.S.) a litre
Note: in fact, our 'cheapest' petrol was an unsolicited gift of a free tankful from an Esso station Manager, in Colombia.

14.5. Oil
Number of oil changes, as routine maintenance: 30
Consumption (excl. changes but including leaks): 158 litres

14.6. Tyres
Total number of punctures en route: 61
New covers bought during journey*:   10
Re-moulded tyres bought *en route:*   2
Second-hand (usually very worn) covers bought: 8
Private gift (Japan) of almost-new snow tyres: 4

*Plus six new tyres (Malojas) on the van on departure.

14.7. Repairs

The repairs (listed) are only those more major and/or inconvenient ones. Routine servicing and maintenance is also not included. The number of times that the engine had to be removed was exceptional, and due mainly to an unhappy chain-reaction, caused by insufficient familiarity by local VW mechanics of the complicated 1700 cc engine we had. (The 1600 cc engine can be taken out and put back in a day by semi-skilled labour. Ours invariably took 2 days, using trained VW labour, just to remove and put back — even in the U.S.).

Damaged track rod	Niger
Front torsion bar. Ball joints	Kenya
Dent in sliding door	Rhodesia
Oil-seals. Eng. mts. Oil cooler (Engine removed)	S. Africa
Valve & piston. Re-bore (Engine removed)	Brazil
Valve + guides. Cylinder head (Engine removed)	Paraguay
Clutch (Engine removed)	Chile
Serious oil leaks (Engine removed)	Bolivia
Eng. cooling system not working (Engine removed)	Peru
Broken distributor part	Ecuador
Re-conditioned block. Ball-joints. Joints. Clutch cable. Magnetic idle jet. Ign. switch + harness.	
Re-plane rear brake drums	USA
Trackrod repair. Part re-wire	Japan
Rear wheel bearing (one)	Singapore
Ign. switch + harness (again)	Thailand
Speedo cable. Bust distributor	India
Second-hand distrib. Oil leaks (Engine removed)	Afghanistan
Appalling oil leaks (Engine removed)	Iran

(The perennial oil leaks were finally cured in a converted open-air cinema by a small one-man outfit in Athens without even removing the engine. It's still o.k. End of saga!)

14.8. Spare parts

From a more extensive list of spare parts used, the following (excluding those on the car on departure) may be of interest:

Engine oil filters 21
Shock absorbers (heavy duty) — ½ of them used in Africa 15
Sets of front disc brake pads 4
Sets of rear brake shoes 2
Light bulbs, 1 side & 1 No. Plate...................................... 2
Condensers 2
Contact points 10
Spark plugs 96
Windscreen wiper blades (pairs) 3
Battery 1

14.9. Weights/Dimensions

Dimensions specified for shipping 15.16 cu m (533 cu ft or 13.3 measured tons)

Weight (No people. Tank ½ full)   2,650 Kg   (January 1973)
Weight (No people. Tank ½ full)   1,995 Kg   (Sept. 1975)

14.10 Personal

Illnesses, other than colds, diahorrea etc: 1 minor op. in South Africa, and 1 broken tooth in Japan.
Attacks, violence, break-ins etc: None.
Troubles with police resulting in fines or jail: None.
Thefts: 1 exterior-mounted air horn.

14.11. Money

Total daily costs (excluding only personal souvenirs) : $19
Total daily costs (excluding souvenirs and shipping) : $12*

NB Shipping does not include roll-on, roll-off ferries, as these are incorporated into normal daily running costs. The figures are for two people and the vehicle. The latter consumed approximately 80% of our expenditure.

14.12. Miscellaneous

Most Northerly point outside Europe: Quebec
Most Southerly point: Tierra del Fuego
Coldest night temperature (Canada, November) :   —23°C
Highest altitude by car (15,889ft) :   4,843m
Total number of colour slides shot: 4,200
Number of Equator crossings: 4
Day missed by crossing Int. date line: Fri 21 Mar 1975

The Authors, Theresa & Jonathan Hewat relaxing in Corfe Castle Village, Dorset, after their record-breaking round the world trip. After 89½ thousand miles, the van looks almost new.

15. Addresses

This small collection of addresses may help as a 'starting point'. If the organisation contacted cannot help you, *always enquire if they know someone who can.* A complete list of all magazines (and addresses) can be found in 'Willings Press Guide' (Published each year, by Thos Skinner Directories Ltd. 01-686 2262) in your local reference library. In some cases we have only given phone nos.

Automobile Association: Head Office: Fanum House, Basingstoke, Hants, RG21 2EA. 0256-20123.

Agfa-Gevaert Ltd: 20 Piccadilly, London W1. 01-734 4854

W.H. Allen & Co. Ltd: 44 Hill Street, W1. 01-493 9471. (Spanish made simple)

American Express (Card Div.): 12 Park Place, SW1. 01-930 4411

American International Underwriters (vehicle insurance for the two Americas): 120 Fenchurch Street, EC3. 01-626 7866

BBC (External Service): Bush Ho. Strand, WC2. 01-240 3456

BMA (Medical Assoc): BMA Ho. Tavistock Sq, WC1. 01-387 4499

Bank of England (Foreign Dept): Threadneedle St, EC2. 01-601 4444.

Birds Eye Foods Ltd: Station Ave. Walton-on-Thames, Surrey. Tel: 28888

Camping Gaz International: 126-130 St Leonards Rd, Windsor. Tel: 55011

Camping shop: Joy and King, 15 Alperton Lane, Perivale, Middx. 997-5653

Chubb Locks Co Ltd: 14 Tottenham Street, W1. 01-637 2377

Cli-Pon Insect Screens Ltd: 495 Ipswich Rd. Trade Est. Slough, Bucks.

Clymer Pubns: 222 Nth Virgil Ave. Los Angeles, Calif 90004. U.S.A.

Diners Club Ltd: 214 Oxford St. London W1. 01-580 2040

Dunlop Group: Dunlop Ho. Ryder St, SW1. 01-930 6700

Encounter Overland: 280 Old Brompton Rd, SW5. 01-370 6845
Expedition Supplies: 280 Old Brompton Rd, SW5. 01-370 6677
Firemaster Ltd (extinguishers): Friendly Pl. Lewisham Rd, SE13

Foreign Office (general enquiries): 01-930 2323
Globe Trotters Club: BCM/Roving, London WC1V 6XX (Worth contacting)
Globetrott-Zentralc Tesch GmbH., Expedition Equipment Suppliers, Kornelius Market 56, 51 Kornelimunster bei Aachen. Tel. 02408-4141.
Goulding, Ian: (Tyre mts for VW fronts): 1 Albert Rd. Notts NG11 6QE
Group Trek travel: Write to Trailfinders for free magazine
HM Customs: Kings Beam Ho. Mark Lane, EC3. 01-283 8911
HMSO (Hints for businessmen): 01-248 5757 (extension 7146)
Hewat, T. & J: 46 Wine Street, Bradford-on-Avon, Wilts, BA15 INS. (S.A.E. — please!)
Insurance: See 'ISIS' (medical) or 'Slugoki' or 'American' (vehicle)
ISIS Insurance: PO Box 9. Gouda. Holland. Netherlands
Katadyne Produkte AG: Industriestr. 27, Wallisellen, Zurich, Switzerland. Tel. Zurich 830 3677
Kodak Ltd: 246 High Holborn, WC1. 01-405 7841
Land Rover: British Leyland, Solihull. Warwickshire. 021-743 4242
Lascelles, Roger: 3 Holl Pk Mans. Holland Pk Gdns, W14 8DY. 01-603 8489
Lucas, Joseph, Ltd: 46 Park St, London W1. 01-493 6793
Maloja Tyres: Ave Appia 1211, Geneva, Switzerland. Tel: 346 061
Maps: Roger Lascelles or Stanford Ltd. (below). (For the free 'Asia Highway' series: Bridgestone Tire Co Ltd Tokyo, Japan)
Met Office (International): Tel: Bracknell, Berks 20242 (ext. 2297)
Michelin Tyre Co Ltd: 81 Fulham Road, SW3. 01-589 1460
Nestle Co Ltd: St Georges Ho. Park Lane, Croydon. 01-686 3333
Optimus Stoves: City Hardware, 20 Goswell Rd. EC1. 01-253 4095
Passport Office: Clive Ho. Petty France SW1. 01-222 8010
Penn Overland Tours Ltd. 01-589 0016
Pilgrims Guide to the Planet Earth: PO Box 1080, S Raphael, Calif. 94902
RAC: PO Box 100. RAC House, Landsdowne Rd. Croydon. 01-686 2314

Red Cross HQ: 9 Grosvenor Crescent, SW1. 01-235 5454

Ross Institute: Keppel Street WC1. 01-636 8636

Safari Water Trtmts Ltd: 28 The Spain, Petersfield, Hants
Tel: 4452

South American Handbook: See 'Trade & Travel Publications
Ltd'

X Slugoki Norman/Campbell Irvine Ltd: 48 Earls Ct Rd. W8
01-937 6981

Stanford Ltd. Edward (Guides/maps/etc.): 12-14 Longacre,
WC2E 9LP. 01-836 1321

Trade & Travel Publications Ltd. Mendip Press, Bath BA1 1EN.
0225 64156 (South American Handbook)

Trail Finders Ltd: 48 Earls Court Rd. W8 6EJ. 01-937 9631

Water Purifiers units: See 'Safari' or 'Katadyne'

VW (GB) Ltd: VW Ho. Brighton Rd. Purley, Surrey CR2 2UE.
01-668 4100

VW (Head Office): Volkswagen. Wolfsberg. West Germany

VW of America Inc: Englewood Cliffs. NJO7632. U.S.A.

Vehicles (2nd hand): NCP Car Park beside Royal Festival Hall,
London

WHO (World Health Organisation) Ave. Appia, Geneva,
Switzerland

Health Insurance.

16. Conversion Tables

1. *Square and cubic measure*

1 sq metre = 10.764 sq ft or 1.169 sq yards. 1 cu centimetre = 0.061 cu inch.
1 cu metre = 35.315 cu ft or 1.308 cu yards. 1 cu yard = 0.765 cu metre.
1 cu foot = 0.028 cu metre.

2. *Capacity*

1 litre = 1.76 pints (0.220 Imperial gallons or 0.264 US gallons).
1 Imperial gallon = 4.546 litres. 1 US gallon = 3.785 litres.
As a general guide, six US gallons equal approximately five Imperial gallons.

3. *Weights.*

1 Kilogram = 2.205 pounds (lbs). 1 pound (lb) = 0.454 Kilograms (Kg)
1 Metric ton (1,000 Kg) = 1.102 short tons or 0.984 long tons.
1 Short ton (2,000 lbs) = 0.097 metric tons. 1 long ton = 1.016 Metric tons.
1 Litre of water weighs 1 Kilogram, and 1 gallon of water weighs 10 lbs.

4. *Distance*

Kilometres (converted to Imperial miles)

1=0.62	6=3.72	11=6.83
2=1.24	7=4.34	12=7.45
3=1.86	8=4.97	13=8.07
4=2.48	9=5.59	14=8.69
5=3.10	10=6.21	15=9.32
16= 9.94	21=13.04	26=16.15
17=10.56	22=13.67	27=16.77
18=11.18	23=14.29	28=17.39
19=11.80	24=14.91	29=18.02
20=12.42	25=15.53	30=18.64

40 = 24.85	100 = 62.14
50 = 31.07	200 = 124.28
60 = 37.28	300 = 186.42
70 = 43.49	400 = 248.56
80 = 49.71	500 = 310.70

For a very approximate guide, convert Km to miles by first dividing by 8 and then multiplying by 5. Miles to Km: Divide by 5 and then multiply by 8. (1Km = 5/8 mile approx.) 1 Metre = 3.281 feet. 1 foot = 0.305 metre. 3 feet = 1 yard. 1 furlong = 1/8 mile.) (Furlongs are still commonly used in India by locals when giving you directions...)

5. *Fuel consumption*

10 mpg = 3.5 kpl	19 mpg = 6.7 kpl
12 mpg = 4.2 kpl	20 mpg = 7.1 kpl
15 mpg = 5.3 kpl	25 mpg = 8.8 kpl
16 mpg = 5.7 kpl	30 mpg = 10.6 kpl
17 mpg = 6.0 kpl	40 mpg = 14.2 kpl
18 mpg = 6.4 kpl	50 mpg = 17.7 kpl

Note: Europeans frequently talk in terms of litres per one hundred kilometres.

6. *Temperature equivalents*

90°C = 194°F	35°C = 95°F
85°C = 185°F	30°C = 86°F
80°C = 176°F	25°C = 77°F
75°C = 167°F	20°C = 68°F
70°C = 158°F	10°C = 50°F
65°C = 149°F	0°C = 32°F
60°C = 140°F	—10°C = +14°F
55°C = 131°F	—20°C = —22°F
50°C = 122°F	—30°C = —31°F
45°C = 113°F	—40°C = —40°F
40°C = 104°F	

To convert Centigrade to Farenheit, multiply by nine over five then add 32.

To convert Farenheit to Centigrade, subtract 32 and then multiply by five ninths.

7. Times (compared with GMT at noon)

Adelaide: 21.30	Istanbul: 14.00
Amsterdam: 13.00	Los Angeles: 04.00
Bombay: 17.30	Melbourne: 22.00
Buenos Aires: 08.00	Mexico City: 06.00
Cairo: 14.00	Moscow: 15.00
Calcutta: 18.00	New York: 07.00 07.00
Cape Town: 14.00	Rio: 09.00
Chicago: 06.00	Tokyo: 21.00

8. *Effects of altitude on engine horsepower (Sea level = 100%)*

1,000 feet (305m): 96%	8,000 feet (2,440m): 74.0%
5,000 feet (1,525m): 83.0%	9,000 feet (2,745m): 71.0%
6,000 feet (1,830m): 80.0%	10,000 feet (3,050m): 68.0%
7,000 feet (2,135m): 77.5%	15,000 feet (4,575m): 53.0%

As a general guide for very high altitude motoring, the timing should be advanced to ascend and retarded on descending — though only fractionally at all times.

Ben Nevis, Scotland, is 4,406 ft (1,343 m). Mont Blanc (Alps) is 15,784 ft (4,814). 4 hours drive West from Lima, Peru, the road rises from sea level to 15,889 ft high.

9.   Tyre pressures (Pounds/sq inch to Kilograms/sq cm)

14 lbs = 0.98	30 lbs = 2.10
16 lbs = 1.12	32 lbs = 2.24
18 lbs = 1.26	36 lbs = 2.52
20 lbs = 1.40	40 lbs = 2.80
22 lbs = 1.24	50 lbs = 3.50
24 lbs = 1.68	55 lbs = 3.85
26 lbs = 1.83	60 lbs = 4.20
28 lbs = 1.96	65 lbs = 4.55

Index (Abbreviated)

The following index is by no means a complete and thorough cross-reference for the entire book. However, it is included to help you to 'home-in' on certain specific subjects mentioned in the book. Where, for example, a water purifier may be mentioned in the anecdotal chapters (3, 4 and 5) it is *not* included in the index.

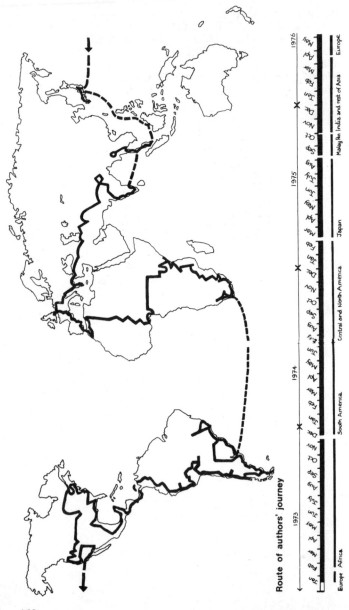

Route of authors' journey

1973 · 1974 · 1975 · 1976

Jan Feb Mar Apr May Jun July Aug Sep Oct Nov Dec Jan Feb Mar Apr May Jun July Aug Sep Oct Nov Dec Jan Feb Mar Apr May Jun July Aug Sep Oct Nov Dec Jan Feb Mar Apr May

Europe | Africa | South America | Central and North America | Japan | Malaysia, India and rest of Asia | Europe